the perfect wedding RECEPTION

STYLISH IDEAS FOR EVERY SEASON

MARIA MCBRIDE-MELLINGER

with

SIOBHÁN MCGOWAN

Photographs by

ROSS WHITAKER

HarperResource

An Imprint of HarperCollins*Publishers*

To my mom, who cheerfully guided
me through my own "I do's."

THE PERFECT WEDDING RECEPTION. Copyright © 2001 by
Maria McBride-Mellinger/mariamcbride.com
Photographs copyright © Ross Whitaker/New York.

HarperCollins books may be purchased for educational,
business, or sales promotional use. For information,
please write: Special Markets Department, HarperCollins
Publishers Inc., 10 East 53rd Street, New York, NY 10022.

FIRST EDITION

Designed by Susi Oberhelman

Printed on acid-free paper

Library of Congress Cataloging-in-Publication Data
McBride-Mellinger, Maria.
    The perfect wedding reception : stylish ideas for
every season / Maria McBride-Mellinger with
Siobhán McGowan. — 1st ed.
      p. cm.
ISBN 0-06-019298-4
    1. Wedding—Planning. I. McGowan, Siobhán. II. Title.
HQ745.M327 2001
395.2'2—dc21   00-044972

01 02 03 04   10 9 8 7 6 5 4 3 2 1

contents

I remember . . .

AFTER ALL these years, the details have blurred a bit. To tell the truth, I barely recall what we ate, when we danced, who caught the bouquet. But there is one thing I'll never forget: My wedding day was a happy one.

It was a sultry afternoon, and the decadent aroma of late summer roses blooming in my mother's garden lulled the guests into a relaxed, dreamlike state. I was only twenty years old, and standing before a fleet of chairs borrowed from our parish hall, I panicked. All assembled—family members, old friends, college mates, favorite teachers, even preschool pals—strained to hear my whispered vows. After months of planning, my wedding day was rushing toward its end. Momentarily, my confidence ebbed. But his steady gaze restored my calm. That I remember.

We put so much energy into perfecting our wedding, planning every last detail to reflect our personality, our heritage, our romantic history. Then the day passes so quickly, too soon, and we discover that what remains is what mattered most in the first place—a pocketful of memories: the sweet smell of my mother's roses or the reassuring look in my husband's eyes. It's funny, but most couples I meet have had the exact same experience. The seemingly endless expenses, the frustrations of scheduling the ceremony and reception site, the challenge of nurturing new relationships, the tortured decisions—indoors or out, disc jockey or band, meat or fish—somehow, magically, they all come together and anchor the day, allowing our thoughts to turn to the truly important issues of love and family. Can the delicate orchestrations of a thousand demands be worth it? Absolutely!

When I thumb through my wedding album, I find myself thanking my mother again and again. I married young, before I had a true sense of style, and before I knew how to plan a successful event. I married with few clear ideas about what I wanted. But my mother was organized, resourceful, determined—my friend. Considering the many weddings I've since created to inspire other couples, I often look back and wonder what sort of choices I might make for myself today.

For years now, I've had a dream job as an editor at *Bride's* magazine. It lets me pretend I'm recreating my own wedding—I live vicariously through, and for, my readers. Every month, I meet with new caterers, chefs, florists, graphic designers, papermakers, calligraphers, and craftspeople. Then I share our ideas with couples planning their own once-in-a-lifetime day. My last book, *The Perfect Wedding*, is intended for those just beginning the process. Its soup-to-nuts format guides

the newly (or about-to-be-) engaged through all the logical questions, from evaluating diamond rings to writing ceremonial vows. Yet I'm often asked, "But how do I put the pieces together in a way that makes sense to me?"

The Perfect Wedding Reception provides the answers. I believe the best way to approach your reception is to think of it as a theatrical production. You're the director, and it's up to you to chose the most appropriate props, fit the staging to the script, and cast the event with players who are talented on their own terms and able to improvise with others.

Four Weddings, Four Rules

As you flip through these pages, you'll see four weddings—one for every season. Custom-tailored to its particular time of year, each exemplifies how the individual elements of a party enhance one another. And frankly, I pulled out all the stops. I searched high and low for fresh ideas that expressed my vision. I consulted with many vendors—some familiar, some new—and collaborated with them to create these four spectacular tableaux. I allowed myself to be inspired by any little item that struck my fancy: teeny-tiny petit-four wedding cakes, an exquisitely azure robin's egg, the glistening crystals of an antique chandelier. Occasionally I indulged my pocketbook, but more often I indulged my senses. The most memorable touches are not necessarily the most expensive.

Indeed, the best weddings are often quite simply styled. At first glance, the four seasonal receptions I've created may appear to be anything but! Yet they all follow my four basic rules. First, their details are dictated by location. Don't try to fight the setting. Go with its flow. For example, it would have been a mistake to force a formal affair at our waterfront summer reception. By working with the warm weather, lush lawn, and pool-side patio, the end result felt fun, comfortable, just right. Showcasing the inherent attributes of a setting can actually save money: a naturally pretty venue needs less makeup.

Second, stick to the season. Let local harvests inform both the menu and the decor. At the autumn reception, we served crisp ciders of pressed apples and pears. In winter, glossy evergreen branches punctuated our pristine snow-white landscape. Adhere to this premise, look to the season for inspiration, and you won't waste precious time, energy, and money in an effort to hunt down hard-to-find items. What's the point of paying exorbitant prices to import flowering fruit-tree branches for a fall wedding when you're already surrounded by glorious foliage?

Third, invite fewer guests. Of course, there's your family, there's his family, and the demands of both of your parents may come into play. But a wedding is an incredibly personal occasion. You don't want to fill your reception hall with folks you hardly know; you want to be able to devote your attention to those you truly cherish. It's an honor for guests to share your milestone moment. Consider it carefully, and as much as possible,

limit your list to the relatives and friends you'd invite to an intimate dinner party.

Finally, make it personal. Celebrate your common interests and distinct differences. What's your favorite food, color, poem, song? How did you and your fiancé meet? What's your cultural background? Take the time to define these elements and weave them into the tapestry that will be your reception. I often recommend that couples create an heirloom to commemorate the event—an engraved sterling silver cake knife, for example, or crystal champagne flutes etched with your initials. Such a keepsake marks the beginning of your journey together as husband and wife, and will serve as a touchstone in the years to come.

Take Time

Once you're engaged, it's easy to get overwhelmed by the excitement. That's to be expected—encouraged, even, and enjoyed. After all, a wedding is not an everyday event. To allow yourself plenty of planning time, I suggest a solid year from proposal to party. In those twelve months, you'll need to scout and schedule locations; decide on a dress for yourself and your attendants and coordinate the menswear as well; print and mail invitations; hire vendors for everything from the food to the flowers; organize the menu and order a cake; arrange for transportation and accommodations; choose the music; plan the honeymoon; and many more details you'd never anticipate. Of course, you'll also want

the chance to change your mind about this or that, which will mean starting over from scratch. Make sure time is on your side.

To draft a realistic game plan, have a frank discussion with your fiancé and determine what you both want and how much you both can afford. (Many couples end up spending more than twice their initial estimate.) Also remember that a courteous host structures an event around her guests. Take precautions to eliminate unnecessary delays, traffic bottlenecks, too-funky foods, and other common irrititants. The reception should closely follow the ceremony, and traveling from one site to the other should be simple.

Details, Details

Because guests will spend a large part of the reception at their tables, all but the most casual events (a cocktail party, for example) should have assigned seats. A good host makes the effort to determine compatible dinner partners. It's a gracious gesture. It's also one of the most complicated tasks for a couple to undertake. Use areas of shared interest as a guideline: seat singles together, or friends from college, or coworkers from the same company. But introduce new people into preexisting "groups" wherever you sense a connection could be made. It requires a bit of a balancing act, so mark your preliminary seating arrangements in pencil, and don't ink the deal until the RSVPs are in and you're absolutely sure.

Basically, the more formal your reception, the more staff you'll need to employ and

the more elements you'll need to coordinate. A formal meal is typically three to five courses, each served with a perfectly paired wine. But to be honest, my favorite weddings are those that blend formal and informal with happy abandon. When done right, they're elegant yet wonderfully relaxed. For example, I strongly advocate centerpieces that allow for eye contact among the guests. Whether beeswax candles clustered in terra-cotta pots substitute for flowers, or low, wide arrangements spill freely over the edges of vintage cake platters, all table decorations should enhance the convivial atmosphere.

Location affects every decision: the number of musicians you can accommodate, the need for valet service, etc. Depending on the amenities offered by the site, you may have to rent not only the flatware and the linens but also the tables themselves. For an outdoor reception, it may even become your responsibility to provide bathrooms. If your location doesn't supply it, you'll have to.

The Creative Process

Request referrals from trusted friends and family members, and query both your contacts and the professionals they recommend in order to determine which vendors best suit your plans. For example, ask if the provider was responsive to suggestions, and compare the final bill to the original estimate. Your primary vendors will be your partners in a creative process. For a few months, you'll be married to them! Hire wisely.

Some couples fear that when they sign a contract with a vendor, they sign over control. Nothing should be further from the truth. If there's one thought I want readers to take away from *The Perfect Wedding Reception,* it's that the best events are the result of successful collaborations. My best ideas are brought to life by the right articulators. After lots of discussion, rumination, and revision, the concepts evolve. The more clearly you see the picture of your proposed reception, the more likely you are to make it real. Looking at the event through someone else's eyes improves your focus.

The receptions that follow are meant to illustrate the many different ways to host a perfect party. Yes, at points they're over the top, but a wedding is literally a dream come true, and the reception is an integral part of its personification. Don't feel compelled to follow any of the four receptions to the letter. Instead, slip into each season and permit yourself to be intoxicated by the possibilities. Think of each as a template, a showcase of how a wedding ought to look when every last detail has been thought through. Take the ideas that touch you, and adapt them to your own reception.

Above all, remember that the most perfect receptions are those at which the true sentiment of the day is plain to see, not hidden behind all the pomp and circumstance. Gather your loved ones around you, and have the time of your life.

MARIA McBRIDE-MELLINGER

sprin

pretty i

Spring intoxicates the senses like no other season. A potpourri of petals paints the landscape in pretty colors, and the heady aromas of tender blossoms perfume the air. Under pollen's spell, the birds and the bees abandon all inhibitions, and we follow suit, surrendering ourselves to whatever dreams may come.

The truest hue of spring is pink—tingeing twilight skies, kissing a rosebud, saturating berry skins.

n HE PINK

There's something at once innocent and suggestive about the shade, making it a perennial favorite of florists and fashion designers. A decorator's delight, it flatters complexions and freshens up interiors. It's unabashedly feminine. Tickled by thoughts of wedded bliss, couples who marry in April or May embrace *la vie en rose.* When planning a springtime reception, take my advice: It's time to think pink!

spring THE ELEMENTS

IN SPRING, flowering branches seem to burst to life overnight, awakening winter's sleepy terrain with color and fragrance. Giddy with the season's fresh starts, couples embark on their own new beginnings. Above all, I wanted our springtime reception to be as spirited as the season—classic, of course, but charming, too. A private garden best provided this contrast, situating nature's wild bouquets within the formal framework of an estate. We happened upon a historic manor house that dated from the turn of the nineteenth century. Its superbly manicured grounds included a Grecian temple, an allée of linden trees, and a walled garden complete with vine-covered trellises. A balustrade accented with cast-stone urns bordered sections of the estate.

Because the beautiful gardens begged to be exposed, we decided on a formal luncheon. The enclosed west porch looked out upon the grounds, and its rosy-toned marble and granite foundation perfectly matched the sophisticated yet winsome pink scheme the bride and I had in mind. (She'd lived in London for many years and, with a wink to royalty, planned to wear a gown fit for a princess—cut from the palest of silks, stitched with sparkling crystals, and topped by a tiny tiara. For his part, the groom dressed to the nines in a dapper morning suit.)

The path from the parking area took guests on a short but oh-so-scenic stroll through the walled garden to the west porch. We served hors d'oeuvres on the red-brick terrace that surrounded the stately mansion. Just a few paces from the porch, a broad beech tree shaded guests with its lush canopy of leaves. As they meandered through the gardens, sipping herbal iced teas and champagne cocktails, guests were greeted by the acoustic tunes of two classical guitarists. At the appropriate moment, a French horn heralded the lunch hour, inviting all up the terrace steps and onto the west porch.

Planning and Preparation

It pays to be prepared for brainstorming sessions. Early in the planning stages, I sat down with Susan Holland, her catering crew, chef Ed Magel, and baker Cheryl Kleinman. For inspiration, I brought along snapshots of the estate and the statuary.

Prior to the meeting, I also assembled a sample table setting out of a multitude of plates. My friend Angèle Parlange, in homage to her great-great-grandmother's Parisian salon and the architecture of her native New Orleans, had designed some delicious raspberry chargers, detailing them with gilded scrolls. I mixed these with chintz dishes and vintage gold-rimmed porcelain side bowls. The assortment conveyed the colorful, eclectic mood I had in mind.

Although I do love to personalize place settings with unique treasures or unusual items rented from prop houses, I rely on party suppliers for almost everything else. Such companies display their products in showrooms, so it's easy to see the selections and experiment with different arrangements. Set your own sample table during your showroom appointment, and when you're satisfied with it, take pictures. As you shop for additional adornments, carry the photos with you to refresh your memory.

Finally, before the meeting, I gathered several fabric swatches in order to illustrate my idea of dressing the tables in different materials. (To give the room a rosy glow, I wanted to alternate pink pinstripes, plaids, and florals.) Armed with all my props, I found it easier to direct the group discussion. I recommend that couples approach such meetings in the same manner. Visuals get the conversation going, and samples that can be passed around and tested in advance express the intended mood of the event in a way mere photographs never can. Fabrics, flatware, place settings, candlesticks, stationery, and flowers all help stimulate the discussion.

The Caterer's Craft ᨑᨠ

Ed, Susan, and the catering crew *(bottom)* were "berry" excited at the prospect of planning a lunch menu that would incorporate spring's ripe fruits, fresh shoots, and tender meats. All caterers maintain a selection of sample menus, usually arranged by event, meal, and season. Looking over the appropriate examples helps kick off the creative process. It's perfectly OK to bring along favorite recipes—I always do—but listen to the chef's suggestions. Quality caterers know from experience what works in different situations, and their sample menus will include courses they cook well. It's particularly wise to follow their advice when a meal is to be prepared off-site—meaning away from their home kitchen. When cooking for a crowd, an amount of advance preparation is inevitable: Some plates can be precooked to a certain stage before an event, then successfully completed on-site; others don't weather the transition as well. It's smarter to serve relatively standard dishes that taste great than to strive for something exotic, only to miss the mark. Caution aside, however, competent chefs should willingly experiment with your suggestions, find a compromise course, and expand their repertoire.

Some caterers suggest sending menu options along with the invitation. I disagree. It's too cumbersome and, frankly, takes the fun out of the event. After all, this isn't a dismal, preprogrammed airplane meal, with a choice of Plan A or Plan B: it's a lavish wedding feast! Either determine the menu in advance, or give guests a chance to select on-site, as they would in a restaurant. Experienced caterers can calculate with astonishing accuracy how many folks in a crowd will prefer fish to meat. Ed's rule of thumb: Have on hand an extra 30 percent of each choice, so that everyone gets exactly what he or she orders. When guests get to choose their entrée, they feel indulged by the individual attention, and it's really no great feat for the caterer—any unused portions can feed the wait staff and other crew members later.

Tablescapes

Although the three-course meal was to be plated, Susan thought it would be fun to welcome guests to their seats with tasty "tablescapes." First, we preset each place with a savory *crottin* of chèvre, drizzled with herbed olive oil and a dash of pink peppercorns, and laid an elegant breadstick baton to one side of the dish. Then we added several juicy starters meant to be shared family style. Bowls of mixed olives, plump cherries, and peeled artichoke hearts with parmesan curls gave guests an excuse to break the ice by asking their neighbor to please pass the appetizing offerings.

Flowers by Phone

Although I usually hire vendors who are based within driving distance of the reception site, it's absolutely doable to work weddings long distance. Don't despair if your ceremony is in Maine but your favorite florist is in Florida! I knew our springtime wedding would be a perfect fit for a pair of floral designers in Dallas—Todd Fiscus and Raegen McKinney of Two Design Group *(opposite, top)*—so I sent them a package that included photos of the location, pictures of centerpieces similar to what I had in mind, and a list of flowers I loved. Of course, I also mentioned the think-pink theme. Todd and I had collaborated together in the past, which made this long-distance relationship easy, but I wouldn't hesitate to hire any vendor who came highly recommended—provided we had some rapport over the phone. In today's world, Web sites, FedEx, and cellular service have made distance almost irrelevant.

Todd ordered the flowers from a Manhattan wholesaler, shipped his tool kit and extra containers ahead of time, and arrived in New York three days before the ceremony for a final prep meeting and a bit of last-minute shopping. He knew exactly what I wanted—lush arrangements teeming with different shapes and shades—and his schedule allowed plenty of time to condition the flowers before the wedding.

Cherry-Colored Cake

Before creating her utterly beguiling, absolutely fabulous wedding cake, Cheryl had just one caveat: no butter cream. I concurred. Our reception was in late spring, when afternoons can turn quite warm. Since the frothy icing quickly melts in heat, couples who insist on butter cream court disaster. I vividly recall a wedding I attended on a hot day in Dallas. The elaborate butter cream bow slid straight off the cake. And let's not even talk about bugs—pesky sugar flies love to bury themselves in sticky butter cream, and an outdoor reception compounds the risk a hundred times over. Instead, Cheryl opted for an icing of fondant. The pliable sugar is easily manipulated but maintains its shape under any condition. I consider it the perfect canvas.

I asked Cheryl to refer to the garden's rose-woven trellises for inspiration and to keep pink as the primary palette. We both wanted a blatantly creative concoction, but we also agreed that a classic three-tiered shape would ground our kooky cake in tradition. Some bakers suggest five tiers or more, but too much of a good thing can turn the cake into a monstrosity, ostentatious and inaccessible. To convey the illusion of height without altering the traditional three-tiered structure, Cheryl simply resized the proportions. Instead of the typical four inches, she made each section about six inches tall. To accommodate the longer slices, we decided to serve dessert on small dinner plates.

Cheryl decorated her three-tiered tower in a pink plaid patterned after one of our tablecloth fabrics, using special utensils to give the icing a plump, quilted look. In homage to the estate's glorious grounds, she dotted the concoction with sweet sugar-blossoms. But the biggest surprise was in the batter, tinted with cherry syrup so that the cake itself was as pink as a rose petal. The whimsical, blushing sponge was the appropriate conclusion to our pink profusion. To complete the presentation, we scattered loose petals across the cake table.

Sweet Somethings

Often, the most memorable aspects of a reception are the small, seemingly last minute, accents—like Cheryl's cheerful cherry batter or the tender rose petals Todd scattered across every blank surface in sight. Look to the season, and brainstorm with your creative crew to come up with extra-special ideas that truly embody the theme of your wedding. Our springtime touches included crystal gems in the bride's bouquet, a custom-mixed pink ink for the place cards, butterfly ornaments affixed to the floral arrangements, and, as the favor, a pretty pink purse made from— imagine this—the couple's old airline tickets.

Maria's Savvy Strategies for Working with Vendors

Book initial appointments at off-hours for pressure-free meetings.

Ask new sources for references—and check them.

Get it in writing: be specific about service, dates, deliveries, and payment.

Don't skimp on staff: heed the advice of your vendors, and hire enough people to insure a smooth event.

Establish a chain of command: make sure that the point person—ideally an event planner or close family member—has cash on hand for gratuities and unexpected expenses.

Provide all vendors with clear directions and contact numbers.

Dress-rehearse the table settings, centerpieces, and menu before the wedding day to guarantee all is right. In case of last-minute emergencies, outline reasonable substitutions.

Allow at least two hours for musicians to set up, and confirm in advance that the space is sufficiently wired for all the instruments.

Finally, be courteous: you're hiring help, not slaves. Acknowledge superior service.

location

grand manors, architects landscaped dramatic outdoor stages for formal gatherings. A reflection pool glimmering with goldfish, set before a graceful stone statue, framed by a classical colonnade, needs little, if any, embellishment for a wedding celebration *(opposite)*. Less glorious grounds can be gussied up with wrought iron gates, mercury-glass gazing balls, elegant water fountains or birdbaths, marble statues or urns, and other garden ornaments available for rent or purchase at floral supply centers, antique boutiques, and flea markets.

Larger-than-life palatial properties easily accommodate a substantial number of guests, but in keeping with my "intimate is always best" rule, we booked for one hundred and, instead of sequestering ourselves in a ballroom, decided to hold the reception on the west porch. The blooming gardens, clearly visible through the windowed walls, naturally became the backdrop, inspiring every aspect of the gathering. After the luncheon, guests strolled out to a columned courtyard, where the wedding cake awaited. Although Diana, goddess of the hunt, stood in perfect, placid repose, Todd and Raegen further adorned her for the event with a glorious garland of flowers *(left)*. The happy revelers danced the rites of spring before this embodiment of strong, feminine spirit.

ESTATES ONCE occupied by barons and earls make the most exquisite reception sites. Imagine: Ornate iron gates swing open to receive your motor car. Down the sloping *champs* you drive, stopping to admire the elaborate facade of the main house before circling back around to the meticulously maintained gardens. On the grounds of such

table settings

LIKE ALICE at the Wonderland tea party, guests were offered an array of luscious treats, presented in a proper, yet whimsical, setting. To create this charming effect, I mix-matched a hodge-podge of colorfully patterned china. Tables were set formally, with place cards, plates and utensils for each course, even a separate pair of salt and pepper shakers per guest, but there was a methodical madness to the arrangements. Chintz dishes sat atop raspberry chargers scrolled with gold swirls *(opposite)*. Gold-trimmed bowls the color of bubble gum offered shavings of savory artichoke and parmesan, while cheerful little compotes contained an assortment of plump olives soaked in citrus and herbs *(left)*. Squiggly seeded breadsticks lined up beside tiny pots of tangy romesco sauce *(center)*— a single baton, conducting the fluid motifs that played across the chargers, also decorated the chèvre *crottin* at each place setting— and bowls of cherries caught the eye with their bright red ripeness *(right)*. Country plaid and pinstripe tablecloths covered tables. A blushing abundance of pink, pink, pink unified all the different elements.

I dreamed of pink table dressings, and fell in love with a trio of complementary

than words, I asked her to draft them quite prominently and to decorate them with a delicate, leaflike swirl that echoed the pattern on the raspberry chargers *(opposite)*. About six inches high, these cards helped guests find their tables. Rendered in the same deep pink ink—a shade mixed expressly for the occasion—the individual place cards coordinated beautifully with the numbered tents *(left)*.

Even the quickest calligraphers need sufficient time to inscribe the table stationery, so I always order the confirmed RSVPs as soon as possible and provide a definitive list of guests ten days prior to the ceremony. Have more than one person proofread your

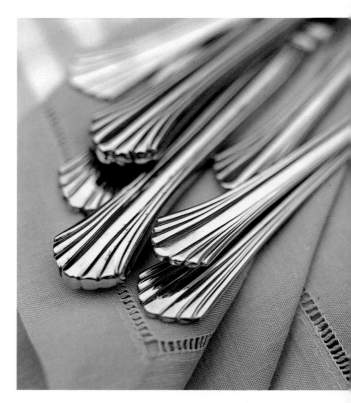

fabrics that transformed my vision into reality. We dubbed the first—a tweedy, houndstoothy plaid—"country couture." The second featured candy cane stripes of pink-and-white taffeta. Embroidered trellises covered the organza overlays that paired with pink linen for the third. I dressed four of our twelve round tables in each fabric for a fresh kaleidoscope of patterns but set all the tables with the same petal-pink linen napkins *(right)*. Cut-crystal goblets and gold flatware underscored the formality.

Calligrapher Caroline Paget Leake scripted tent cards on the same fine stock she'd used for the place cards. Knowing that numerals are easier to read from a distance

spelling before you send the names off to the calligrapher, and never rely on phone messages to communicate—the margin for error is too great. Instead, play it safe by providing the artist with a clearly typed or carefully hand-printed list.

To underscore the springtime garden scheme, I rounded up dozens of whimsical white wrought-iron garden chairs *(opposite)*. Since they may be hard to find, especially in bulk, consider alternating them with traditional white wooden ballroom chairs, which convey the same airy, outdoors feeling.

In keeping with the boundless energy of the season, we chose to forego vases altogether, and instead arranged the flowers on footed porcelain cake plates. Stems were secured in oasis squares set atop these mini-pedestals, and the flat platters permitted the blossoms to spill forth over the edges. Each pretty centerpiece featured a pastel rainbow-burst of color: rich pink peonies, verdant fern fronds, blushing roses, fragrant French lilacs, pliant sweet pea vines, and blooming dogwood branches. Although the raised plates lifted the bouquets above the table's surface, their wide, low profile allowed for easy eye contact between seated guests.

As a finishing touch, we carpeted the floor with soft petals plucked from less-than-perfect flowers or those with broken stems. When guests arrived, they were left to ponder if perhaps they had just missed the processional of the Faerie Queene, her handmaidens scattering blossoms before her every step.

refreshments

glass flutes. Sterling straws anchored by silver hearts make mesmerizing swizzle sticks.

Such a sweet drink deserves a scent-sational garnish. Almost any edible flower, herb, or fruit will do. We filled plum-colored lotus bowls with mint sprigs, raspberries, lemon zest, rosebuds, geranium petals, and snapdragon blossoms *(left)*. Although our choices were based first and foremost on their pretty appearance, we were also charmed by the Victorian notion that plants conveyed individual characteristics. For example, the raspberries represented gentleness; the geraniums offered comfort; the lemon zest, fidelity; and the rosebuds, innocence. Floral ornaments should float on the surface of the sugary liquid. They are not meant to be swallowed. For safety's sake, be sure all toppings are pesticide-free and thoroughly rinsed.

Out in the garden, the sun had concocted other refreshing tonics. Peach blossom punch, elder flower water, hibiscus and chamomile teas—the fragrance of fruits and flowers flavored an assortment of pastel infusions *(overleaf)*. For each we used one heaping teaspoon of leaves per cup of water, then let the teas steep in the sun for about four hours. Quaint decanters and decorative pitchers, tied with thin ribbons, gold wire, and herbal sprigs, held the sparkling ades.

TO CAST A MAGIC SPELL over bride, groom, and guests, bartenders mixed a mysterious pink potion. The elixir, an old-fashioned sour cherry shrug, combines sparkling wine or water with sour cherry syrup, which gives it a romantic rosy hue *(opposite)*. To better admire the bubbles, serve the fizzy brew in elegant crystal or etched-

the menu

Spring Menu

HORS D'OEUVRES

Jumbo Lump Crab on Avocado
Ceviche with Chopped Tomato and
Lime Juice on Noodle Crisp

Smoked Salmon with Chives and
Pickled Ginger on Wasabi Sticky Rice

Vietnamese Chicken in Rice-Paper
Roll with Peanut Mirin Sauce

Mango with Greek Yogurt and
Chervil in Sesame Seed Barquette

FIRST COURSE

Warm Asparagus with Black
Truffles and Poached Quail Egg in
Black Truffle Vinaigrette

ENTREE

Seared Salmon Bouillabaisse with
Saffron Potatoes, Fava Beans, Haricots
Verts, Poached Fennel, and Black Olives
or
Lamb Pot-au-Feu in Roasted-Garlic
Fumet with Herbed Spaetzle and Baby
Spring Vegetables

SWEET BITES

Raspberry with Tarragon Cream
Honeydew Lemon Sorbet
Crushed Strawberries Robiola
in Phyllo Tuilles

DESSERT

Wedding Cake with Panna Cotta

AFTER WINTER'S hibernation, taste buds reawaken to the flavors of spring's young shoots, baby fruits, fresh fish, and tender meats. For the reception's brunch, I wanted to balance formality with lighter fare intrinsic to the season. The brunch would be the day's main meal, so it had to be substantial, but not so rich as to be soporific. I didn't want to incite a siesta, with guests dozing off in their lawn chairs! My aim was to begin the meal with foods that felt breakfasty and finish with a more traditional entrée. Of course, in keeping with our fanciful springtime theme, it was equally important that the ingredients reflect the season and entertain the eye.

Hors d'Oeuvres

Bride and groom were fond of travel—they'd fallen in love while sailing the Caribbean—so we decided our hors d'oeuvres should reflect the tastes of places they'd visited together. Lump crab brought them back to their fateful boat trip: shreds of the tasty meat topped a ceviche of avocado grounded by a wedge of quick-fried wonton. Small tomato chunks, splashed with lime juice, gave the small bite a tangy boost *(opposite)*.

Smoked salmon, that reliable brunch favorite, got a facelift for the occasion. We trimmed slices into neat disks that sat like lids

on squat cylinders of wasabi-flavored sticky rice *(top)*. The resulting sushi redux, graced with pink rose petals and chive sprinkles, reminded the couple of their travels along the Alaskan coast.

In anticipation of a honeymoon adventure to the Far East, shredded chicken was wrapped in rice paper, then sliced into modified Vietnamese spring rolls *(center)*. Creamy peanut sauce invited diners for a dip.

Floating in a golden salver, a battalion of sesame seed barquettes carried sharp spoonfuls of rich yogurt *(bottom)*. Mango ribbons sweetened the punch, and bits of chervil brought a taste of Greece to the tropics.

For the first course, we were torn between a green salad, with all its seasonal freshness, and something a little richer, like brunch's traditional eggs Benedict. Ed suggested a Solomonic solution: a perfectly poached quail egg cradled in a nest of warm asparagus *(opposite)*. Black truffle vinaigrette and cracked black pepper spiced the spears, and buttered brioche toast points brought back childhood memories of breakfast.

Entrée

After guests had taken their seats and served themselves from the tablescapes—artichoke shavings with parmesan curls, assorted herbed olives, chèvre *crottin* sprinkled with pink peppercorns, and seeded breadsticks—waiters approached with an oaky chardonnay and a simple inquiry: Lamb or salmon? Both entrées were plated with an assortment of spring

Berry Bites ᨒ

Toward the end of the brunch, a swing band struck up some tunes on the terrace. Waiters circulated indoors and out, offering each guest a gilded, shell-shaped saucer with three sweet bites: a raspberry tucked in tarragon cream, a scoop of honeydew-lemon sorbet, and a spoonful of crushed strawberry robiola *(opposite)*. Each was wrapped in flaky layers of phyllo pastry. These fruity morsels refreshed guests after the midday meal and left just enough room for the fabulous wedding cake.

vegetables. Seared filet of salmon soaked in a savory bouillabaisse of fava beans, poached fennel, haricots verts, black olives, and saffron-flavored potatoes *(above)*, while braised lamb shanks and thick rib chops rested on a bed of herbed spaetzle, surrounded by bright carrots and crunchy beets *(right)*. For added charm, I'd intentionally rented five different gold-rimmed plate patterns from a collector of vintage porcelain. When guests looked at the amusing mix of dishes on the table, they felt as if they'd come home to Grandma's for the holidays, and she'd pulled out all her favorite china to accommodate them.

the cake

first slice exposed an intense pink interior! Cheryl baked layers of classic white cake but tinted the batter with essences of cherry. Vanilla cream filling helped the rosy bricks stick together. To accompany the cake, Susan and Ed designed trifle towers striped with strawberry-rhubarb gelatin *(below)*. Little leaves of royal icing sprouted from the rooftops of the light, custardlike panna cotta.

MAD ABOUT PLAID and thinking pink, Cheryl whipped up a whimsical wedding cake. At its crown, frosted rosebuds overwhelmed a minty sugar urn *(above)*. Spiral ribbons of gum paste covered the green vase. Cheryl iced the cake in white fondant, embossing it with a tool that gives the frosting a quilted appearance. The checkerboard pattern was then hand-painted with a wash of pink. The resulting picnic plaid matched our "country couture" tablecloths to a T.

The cake was crazy enough on the outside. Imagine the guests' delight when the

the details

NOTHING IS QUITE as stately as a monogram. I asked calligrapher Caroline Paget Leake to create a three-letter motif in a contemporary variation of classic copperplate, which dates from the seventeenth century. The modern feel of her fluid script counterbalanced the monogram's formality *(right)*. Tradition dictates that a couple should not share a monogram until after they are wed, but because the bride's and groom's last names both began with the same letter, and because they were hosting their reception together, it seemed right to bend the rules a bit.

The Invitation

The monogram, in gold ink, marked the cover of the invitation, and I suggested to the couple that they order blank cards with the same engraving for their thank-you notes. The primary, up-front cost of an imprimatur comes from the labor and materials used to make the original die, a metal plate etched with the design. During the printing process, this plate is used to impress a pattern into the paper, resulting in raised lettering. The plate's value rests in its reusability.

As always, the details reflected many other elements of the reception. The gold of the ink echoed the gold of the flatware, and the vertical fold on the invitation made for a

card as elegant as our "elongated" wedding cake. We opted for ecru bond and printed the announcement on tissue-thin sheets of paper in a matching color. It was inserted between the covers along with an RSVP card. Hinting months in advance at the pink theme of the planned reception, we lettered the RSVP card and return envelope in the same hand-mixed rosy ink that would later be used for place cards and table numbers.

A Tiny Tote Bag

Because bride and groom were avid travelers, about to embark on a journey to the Far East, they wanted to send their friends home with a little something that spoke to their sense of adventure. I asked artisan Marie-Celeste Edwards to construct a teensy tote bag from handmade paper—in pink, *bien sûr (page 48)*. Papermaking is a wondrous art—almost anything can be turned into pulp: old T-shirts, baby togs, used books. Prompted by my suggestion that they contribute personal mementos to the process, the couple gave Marie-Celeste airplane tickets from their trips together and a threadbare oxford shirt they used to share. Both became part of the pulp.

Milky glass beads looped on gold wire studded the handles of the finished sachets. The couple tucked a simple thank-you into each purse, along with a few rose petals. Guests could add their own souvenirs of the day—their place cards, wedding programs, and perhaps a flower from the table's centerpiece.

The Bride's Bouquet

For the formal daytime ceremony, the groom sported a morning suit, complete with a classic cut-away coat that was cropped slightly shorter than the typical swallowtail style worn at night. Pinstriped charcoal trousers supported a bibbed white shirt and gray vest. Ascots or striped cravats traditionally complete the ensemble, but we wanted to freshen up the look. The small pink-patterned check

of a beautiful silk tie did the trick. For a finishing touch, we pinned a protea boutonniere on the jacket's lapel *(page 50, left)*.

Todd and Raegen fashioned different combinations of the same colorful flowers—garden roses, grape hyacinth, tight lilac spires, and sweet pea—for each of the three bridesmaids' bouquets *(page 50, center)*. Satin ribbon, braided and buttoned around the base, created smooth handles for the maid of honor to hold *(page 50, right)*. In contrast, the bride's bouquet subtly blushed from one shade of pink to the next—Priscilla roses to lily of the valley to sweet pea *(page 51)*. Diamanté dewdrops encircled the arrangement. Sprouting from stems of fine golden wire, these sparkling crystals—known to exude healing energy—mirrored the smaller stones on the bodice of the satin bridal gown.

A Floral Focal Point

Happily, handsome spaces such as the glass-enclosed, limestone-pillared porch where the reception was held require little in the way of extra adornment. Because the paned walls made us feel as if we were sitting in the garden, I didn't want to obscure the view with lots of large arrangements. I do, however, believe in the power of a single, striking focal point. I'd found a stately—and weighty—stone pedestal at an antique garden-ornament shop. Its weathered appearance resembled that of the balustrade bordering the grounds. Inspired by the mercury-glass gazing ball planted out in the garden, Todd and Raegen

created an indoor twin from verdant hydrangea *(opposite)*. We tied the giant popcorn-ball of a bouquet with satin and organza streamers that spilled to the floor, where they pooled in silky puddles at the column's base.

Primitive cultures believed that demons lurked underground. To protect newlyweds from the subterranean spirits, they scattered petals along the bridal path, using beauty as a

For the bride and groom, Todd and Raegen wrapped heart-shaped wreaths of fern fronds and sweet peas around the metalwork of the chair backs to create flowering thrones fit for Titania and Oberon *(page 53)*.

Regal urns on the stone parapet surrounding the terrace marked the entranceway to the west porch. To define the parameters of the reception area, we filled these finials with cascading flowers *(opposite)*. Blooming peonies, tulip cups, feathery ferns, and poppy

weapon to ward off evil. With a wink to the old tales, we carpeted the floor with flowers. It was as if a gentle breeze had brought rose petals to rest under our feet.

Blossoms and herbs have always been regarded as harbingers of goodwill. Like our ancestors, we looked to nature to bestow her blessings on the reception. We garnished the backs of the iron garden chairs with pittosporum sprigs and hydrangea florets and dressed the seats with miniskirts of bright pink silk.

pods shot forth from the urns like fireworks from a cannon.

It's essential that flowers suit the scale of their setting. To achieve the proper balance, follow this simple rule of thumb: Make the arrangements at least as tall and as wide as the container itself. After establishing the height— as we did with delphinium, dogwood, and lupine—fill out the shape with other flowers. For the springtime tableaux, Todd and Raegen loosely grouped the blossoms by type, so that on one side, an explosion of lacy astilbe spilled over the edges of the urn *(page 54, bottom)*, while at the back, a cluster of lush peonies turned their faces toward the sun *(page 54, top)*. At the base of each urn, slabs of moss cushioned the soft skin of baby peaches. The sight of a stilled butterfly (procured at a naturalist's shop) rewarded those who couldn't resist a closer look. From afar, the arrangements appeared profuse and majestic; face to face, they became miniature vignettes, condensing the wealth of flowers to be found in the gardens beyond.

When the couple left their reception to change into traveling clothes, I alerted the staff. By the time the two were about to depart, three waiters stood on the balcony above the main entrance, at the ready with baskets of rose petals. As husband and wife exited the mansion, a fragrant rain anointed their fresh start. Rumbling in the drive, a chauffeured roadster, its classic lines a match for the stately mansion, whisked the Mr. and Mrs. away on another grand adventure. ✍

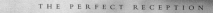

TABLE ACCENTS

The right table setting for a reception coaxes friends to come, sit, and stay awhile.
It's welcoming. Guests will spend about two hours anchored to their temporary
port, so no detail can afford to be neglected. The basic elements of a standard
setting include flatware, stemware, plates, and linens. For well-dressed tables, add to
the list place cards, condiments, a centerpiece, and the all-important elbow room.
No one likes to feel cramped, but too much space between seats can have the
reverse effect, making the table seem vast and
vacant. Allow about twenty-four inches per
place setting. A table sixty inches in diameter
can comfortably seat eight to ten guests; a
forty-eight inch round accommodates six.

Strike a match and spark a flame—it's the most simple way to add drama to any event. For a spring wedding, I clustered trios of pastel tapers in squat pewter containers. To complement the playful mix of colors, baker Jan Kish wired together short strands of sugar flowers. Easy to manipulate, the wired garlands wrapped around the base and climbed up each wax column like vines on a trellis. Butane torches make the task of lighting dozens of candles less daunting.

Strive for comfort, but also for style. Tables
should match the mood of your reception—
indeed, of your union. An expertly coordinated
collection of sterling and crystal conveys the formality of an affair, while more
whimsical accents, such as rainbow-colored candles or mismatched napkins,
balance the importance of the occasion with a bit of humor. And look for ways
to individualize your dining room. Search out candles in surprising shapes, substitute traditional wine glasses with generous etched tumblers, inscribe place cards
with memorable calligraphy, and garnish the plates with a take-home treat—decadent chocolates or a luxurious ribbon wrapped around each linen square.

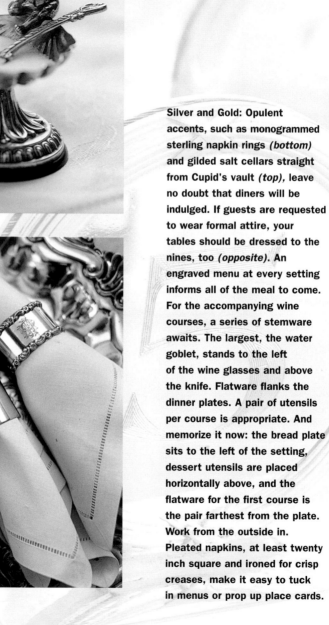

Silver and Gold: Opulent accents, such as monogrammed sterling napkin rings *(bottom)* and gilded salt cellars straight from Cupid's vault *(top),* leave no doubt that diners will be indulged. If guests are requested to wear formal attire, your tables should be dressed to the nines, too *(opposite).* An engraved menu at every setting informs all of the meal to come. For the accompanying wine courses, a series of stemware awaits. The largest, the water goblet, stands to the left of the wine glasses and above the knife. Flatware flanks the dinner plates. A pair of utensils per course is appropriate. And memorize it now: the bread plate sits to the left of the setting, dessert utensils are placed horizontally above, and the flatware for the first course is the pair farthest from the plate. Work from the outside in. Pleated napkins, at least twenty inch square and ironed for crisp creases, make it easy to tuck in menus or prop up place cards.

"Semiformal" sometimes seems like a confusing contradiction in terms. Is the occasion stately? Casual? Actually, it's both. But when it comes to table settings, it's better to err on the side of formal and add the informality through tiny personal touches. For example, place cards are de rigueur, but the style of lettering can vary. Pine cones sprayed in silver make whimsical card holders for a holiday wedding *(top)*. Calligrapher Anna Pinto used silver ink to inscribe names in what she calls casual copperplate. To match a summer bride's blue tulle ball gown, calligrapher Stephannie Barba created paper napkin-bands in a similar shade and labeled them with the couple's monogram *(opposite)*. Blue-and-white transferware continued the theme. Semiformal tables may be set with less silver and stemware, and for a dash of charm at each setting, I encourage the use of quirky elements—like my shiny aluminum stone knife-rest *(bottom)*.

The heart that loves is always young

Informal does not equal boring: no matter how relaxed your reception, it should still feel special. For an afternoon brunch served family style with open seating, I asked Anna Pinto to pen a keepsake message for each guest *(above)*. Threaded at one end with a white silk ribbon, it became a perfect bookmark for after the party. Pastry chef Newton Pryce marked the romantic missives with delicate tuille valentines. After covering tables in plain cotton cloths, I asked Stephannie Barba to paint a pretty floral design on the corners of bright white butcher-paper squares *(opposite)*. She used watercolors and, in lieu of place cards, wrote the name of the guest above each plate. So-easy arrangements of fresh grass ringed with flowers replace elaborate centerpieces. Just remind your guests: Please don't eat the daisies!

M is for Marriage: I threaded tin letters with thin satin ribbons, then laced them around neatly folded napkins for a less formal take on the traditional ring. A sprig of lily of the valley seasons the dish *(opposite)*. At a more formal affair, wide satin ribbons monogrammed by Emily Marcello wrapped iridescent, nubby silk napkins *(above)*. Or use beautiful baubles of Venetian glass to decorate the linens. I love to knot napkins with ornaments intended to be taken home as wedding favors: Dorian Webb designed these gorgeous orbs. To save time, iron, fold, and trim napkins days in advance.

Technically, place cards can rest almost anywhere by the plate. Just follow my two caveats: make cards easy to read and, in case of last-minute changes, easy to alter. Why not keep the smallest of gatherings on a first-name basis *(opposite)*. Calligrapher Maria Thomas embellished the extra space with enthusiastic swirls. Brides blessed with good penmanship can buy blanks and write their own cards *(bottom)*—prepare for a few mistakes and pick up extras. Because a couple needs more than one element of stationery—Invitations, place cards, thank-yous—it's smart to employ a unifying motif *(top)*. Once almost a lost art, letterpress, a technique that involves imprinting paper with an image, is enjoying a renaissance, thanks to artisans such as Julie Holcomb. She custom-designs patterns, like these regal leaves or the lighthearted wedding cake, that can be reproduced in any shade of ink on almost any weight of paper.

When it comes to calligraphy, select a style that corresponds to the formality of your affair. I admire the old-world flourish of Spencerian script *(top)*. In homage to past eras, Bernard Maissner penned his cards in rich brown ink on ecru bond. The slightly burnished palette perfectly underscored the classical influence. Traditionalists inscribe cards horizontally, but for a semiformal reception, why not stack names? Stephannie Barba filled each frame with graceful lines, and I anchored the cards with interlocking rings of gilded chocolate—a sweet metaphor for marriage *(opposite)*. At informal weddings, almost anything goes. Marie-Celeste Edwards, a papermaker with a sense of whimsy, crafted her place cards with custom watermarks *(bottom)*. Stephannie echoed the fanciful curls of the cursive hearts in her script. To emphasize an informal atmosphere, use inks in gentle hues, like moss green or cerulean blue.

Magdalena & Steven

A Scarlet Emblem: Many brides love the look of sealing wax and use it to secure their invitations, but the stamp often shatters en route, spoiling the special effect. Instead, I suggest saving seals for the reception. Jennifer Viviano, a graphic designer who works with mixed mediums, matched place cards to menus with a monogrammed ruby mark *(opposite)*. Textured paper offers another elegant option. Zelda Tannenbaum creates her stationery by embossing bits of lace *(above)*. To eliminate the need for place cards, Stephannie Barba personalized the top of each menu cover.

Table Labels: Unless open seating is the order of the day, tables need to be numbered. In the rush to finalize the menu, the music, and so on, couples often overlook little things like table numbers, but it's exactly this sort of detail that can transform a reception into a truly unique event. Ginger Kilbane, an aficianada of hotel silver, markets a line of handsome reproductions, such as stately engraved silver-plated circles *(opposite)*. For the marriage of two schoolteachers, I found a set of country chalkboards and asked Stephannie Barba to decorate the slates with pastel colors and childlike drawings *(top)*. Superduper sugar artist Steven Klc crafted art-nouveau-style numbers out of pulled sugar *(bottom)*. The delicate wildflowers bloomed across the dining room of a midsummer night's reception.

EAT, DRINK & BE MARRIED

Betsy & Chad
A True Lovers Knot

Nantucket June

I get a kick out of sprucing up strictly utilitarian fare like coasters. By protecting tables from the natural sweat of chilled cocktails, they serve a practical purpose, but that doesn't mean they can't also be fun to look at. Basic paper doilies come in dozens of sizes and styles, and the blank space in the center begs to be personalized *(opposite)*. Stephannie Barba penned the first names of bride and groom in indelible ink, but it would have been just as amusing to detail the doilies with a rubber stamp. I always keep an eye out for interesting ways to showcase monograms *(bottom)*. Trimmed into disks, then initialed and bordered with fluid vines by Stephannie, midweight paper became a secure base for slippery stemware. With wood-blocks and letterpress artwork, Purgatory Pie Press prints charming, tongue-in-cheek sayings on heavy-duty stock to create thick coasters guests will want to keep *(top)*.

summ

bright

By June, the sun reaches the peak of her powers, and no one can resist her charms. Defenseless against the heat, the only option is to relent. Relax. Slip off your shoes, stroll through the sand, dip a toe in the onrushing tide. It's summer. Dive in. The water's fine.

I delight in the seductive warmth of this easy season, when long, languid days gently glide into balmy, moonlit nights. Tradition may call for the formality of

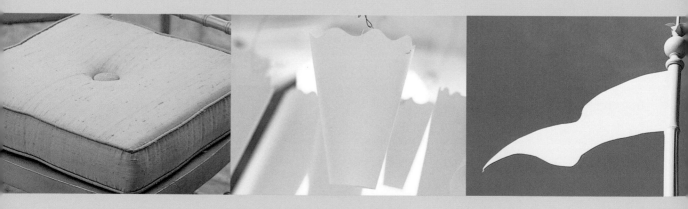

and SUNNY

an all-white wedding, but the season has so much more to offer. I am most fond of seaside receptions, when offshore winds soothe the sun's sultry caress. Envision a barefoot bride, her cheeks flushed with excitement, dancing a samba under the stars. Her loved ones surround her, peeking in and out of colorful cabanas scattered across the lawn. Such splendor in the grass can occur only in summertime.

summer
THE ELEMENTS

ROWS OF SUNNY, striped cabanas lining beaches from Deauville to Miami; primitive thatched parasols peppering Caribbean shores; staunch canvas tents sheltering nomadic bedouins from desert sandstorms; even the colorful carnival canopies of Venice and San Paulo: these iconic structures inspired our summer reception. The bride and groom had met as kids at sleep-away camp, and they wanted their wedding to capture the carefree spirit of those adventurous outdoor days.

A family farm bordering Chesapeake Bay, its acres trimmed with thin strips of pebbled beaches, provided the perfect site. Cattails and Queen Anne's lace fringed the property; weeping willows spilled their leafy waterfalls onto the soft grass; and, like an ambassador from the natural world, the occasional egret made an appearance. Long ago, the groom's uncle had built a simple swimming pool near the water's edge. The surrounding slate-stone patio and manicured lawns made the spot ideal for a relaxed gathering of approximately a hundred guests. Conveniently, a nearby pool house offered everything essential to orchestrating the event, from electricity to plumbing.

Gifted with the spectacular vista afforded by the waterfront, I decided to design our reception in a way that would showcase

the seashore. I certainly didn't want to compete with the scenery. Instead, I aimed to incorporate exotic elements into everything from the cocktails to the centerpieces, in order to evoke an atmosphere that would transport the party to a tropical paradise. So my thoughts turned to tents: By crafting one central tent for the members of the wedding, surrounding it with smaller, parasoled tables, setting the cake under its very own baldachin, and planting a few chaise lounges by the bay, my team and I aimed to create a festive outdoor theater. The open, airy tents and umbrellas would provide shade for the players without obscuring the placid landscape.

To execute this elaborate tableau, I expanded my usual support crew by two. In addition to florist Preston Bailey, baker Margaret Braun, and caterer Peter Callahan, I brought on board Geoff Howell, a master set designer, and Todd Moore, a fabric specialist. Over the course of two months, we met every two weeks to orchestrate our game plan. While I knew each individual's style, my teammates were strangers to one another, so I asked them all to bring portfolios to the first meeting. It's important for your group of professionals to be familiar with one another's range. It makes for better relationships, it sparks creative concepts, and it frequently leads to

future endeavors. As soon as we wrapped our wedding, this bunch had already begun collaborating on other events.

In preparation for our first meeting, I skimmed old magazines, tearing out any pictures I could find of beach cabanas and tropical huts. I also brought fabric swatches close in shade and texture to my ideal. Then, after a round of introductions, I began to paint a word picture of my fantasy reception. The evening was to sail away on the strains of sultry bossa nova songs; splashes of citrus would color everything from the cake to the tablecloths; fringed parasols and floating lanterns would ornament an otherwise open lawn; an assortment of fresh seafood and tropical fruit would make for a satisfying, but light, meal. All in all, the day would be elegantly casual, as epitomized by the barefoot bridal party—bridesmaids wore white bathing suits, skirted with mellow-yellow or kiwi-green batik sarongs *(right)*.

Bamboo and Tropical Blossoms

Thrilled at the chance to bring such a fun affair to life, the team got right down to business—designating responsibilities, outlining a timetable, and mapping a floor plan. Preston, free from the constraints of traditional reds

and pinks, built his bouquets around a few striking flowers in yellow, green, even borderline blue: velvet cattails, exotic cymbidium orchids, buttonlike celadon chrysanthemums, beaded strands of misty, minty amaranth, and clusters of verdigris blueberries *(center)*. But he didn't overlook the practical in his choices—orchids thrive in humidity and would travel well in the hot weather.

Bamboo quickly became an indispensable design element. Its deep green casing grounded all the other flowers, its cylindrical tubes made excellent containers for the centerpieces, its stem length could be trimmed to accommodate different purposes, and its tropical look perfectly fit the theme.

Arrivals and Departures

Because we'd be traveling to a relatively remote location, we couldn't afford to forget anything. We made a packing list and checked it twice. Certain items could be constructed in advance and transported, but others had to be assembled on site, so we accounted for every last nut, bolt, and nail, and rented extra tables for the crew to use during installation.

When planning a wedding, remember that a reception also has to be dismantled. Buffet stations must be broken down, extra food refrigerated, and trash properly discarded. Professionals leave a site just as they found it. Discuss these tasks with your vendors well in advance of the event, so that the team can allot an appropriate amount of time, equipment, and staff for the job. We calculated two days for setup, one for breakdown, and worked out an arrival schedule that included accommodations for the crew.

Poolside Cocktails

Caterer Peter Callahan *(opposite, top)* agreed that the menu should incorporate fresh seasonal fare—an East-meets-West, retro-meets-modern taste of the tropics. He had the brilliant idea of using minigrills—a twist on the popular pupu platters of the sixties—at a bamboo-supported buffet station offering hot and cold hors d'oeuvres. The hip hibachis became the sizzling cornerstones of our "fire-and-ice" concept. Their vintage vibe fit the reception's retro feel, and the participation they required—as guests chose the components of their kabobs—got people talking at the informal outdoor gathering. A pit of roaring coals, manned by several cooks, grilled the main course of red snapper.

A Painted Cake

I've found that just about everyone I love to work with in the event business is an artist of some sort. Margaret Braun is no exception *(opposite, bottom)*. A baker and a painter, she's renowned for tinting her cakes with one-

⊸◷⊸ More Tips ⊸◷⊸ for Summerizing Soirees

Collect shells, wash well, and scatter about place settings. Use large scallops as salt and pepper cellars; thread sand dollars around napkins with sea grass.

Shelter outdoor candles from summer winds: plant them in oversize glass goblets filled with an inch of sand.

For a raw bar, commission an ice block or freeze cubes that incorporate flowers, shells, or other whimsical elements.

Craft flowering frames or freestanding screens. Build frames out of two-by-fours, then stain, paint, or wrap the wood with thin-gauge sheet metal. Or stretch chicken wire across each frame and staple, then fill the center with fresh, silk, or paper flowers.

Whitewashed kitchen tables with pretty pedestals make fresh reception tables.

For modern, minimalist centerpieces, cluster vases in quads, then fill with water tinted a deep blue: a half-teaspoon of food coloring does the trick.

Perfect summer fabrics: gingham, tropical prints, blue-and-white ticking, quilts, cotton duck, crisp linen, lace.

Keep parasols on hand so guests can shield themselves from strong rays.

Replant daisy or sweetheart rose shrubs in chintz pitchers or enamelware buckets for casual centerpieces.

of-a-kind colors she mixes herself, then decorating them with gilded sugar fixtures. I describe her distinctive look as baroque pop art. For our summer reception, Margaret suggested we construct a cake with a sleeker silhouette. By stacking six tall tiers, and accenting each layer with gilt braids and baubles, she created an ornate, edible obelisk. The pyramidlike shape mirrored that of the floral centerpiece on the bridal party's table, and the icing, washed in pastel yellows and greens, matched the reception's overall palette.

Camping at Water's Edge

Whenever I want to build something fanciful and, frankly, a bit over the top, I call Geoff Howell *(bottom)*. There's nothing he can't do. I explained to him my vision of a wandering tribe that had set up camp by the water's edge. Bride and groom would occupy the tent of honor, and their guests would surround them, seated at smaller, parasoled tables scattered across the lawn. Primitive lanterns hanging from bamboo branches would mark the territory where, for one night, the clan would celebrate a wedding ritual.

Geoff loved the idea of a traveling feast. To make my romantic oasis a reality, he designed oversize umbrellas with scalloped edges and open, airy tents that resembled colorful cabanas. The center of the partyscape, the bridal tent, had to be big enough to

accommodate a round table for eight. Geoff stitched the roof out of water-resistant canvas and painted it a celery green. He then crowned this broad awning with a smaller, pointed tent the color of marigold. From its peak, we pitched an elegant pennant, and for an extra bit of exotic, old-world charm, we curtained the sides of the bridal tent with panels of color-washed, sheer cotton gauze.

But as the saying goes, you can't build castles in the air. To elevate this fantasy tent, we needed a support structure. Preston commissioned an ironworker to weld an armature to our measurements. On location, Geoff fastened the canvas fabric to the metal pyramid, which was then mounted on attachable legs.

The guest tables seated four. Each was shaded by a parasol similar in style to the bridal tent. These bright umbrellas opened on poles made from—what else?—bamboo.

We draped all the tables in shimmering shantung—the nubby luxe texture caught the late-afternoon light. After Todd *(opposite, top)* had found the right kiwi-cantaloupe colors to match our scheme, he designed two different types of tablecloths. Short, two-tone squares skirted the poolside cocktail tables, while long, liquid rounds washed over the dinner tables, puddling in soft folds on the grass *(opposite, center)*. For the bridal tent, Todd stitched a cloth from several pieces of silk fabric to create a playful pinwheel of color.

Maria's Money-Saving Ideas for a Tight Budget

Prioritize. Decide what you love, what you need, what you can live without.

Smaller is better. Small guest lists allow for more style splurges. Can't cut your number? Then skip the meal, and just serve cake and champagne.

Keep an eye out for off-season or off-night bargains.

Hosting the reception in a restaurant saves money otherwise spent on party rentals.

Purchase wine directly from local vineyards or liquor merchants. Ask if unused cases can be returned. Serve a limited number of beverages—sparkling water and white wine, for example.

Avoid time-consuming details: you're paying for labor as well as materials.

Stick to seasonal fruits and flowers— abundant produce is more affordable.

Basics—classic white tablecloths, simply patterned flatware, and plain porcelain—are better priced.

Hire a reputable event planner who can get the best bang for your buck.

Plan in advance. Avoid rush decisions by researching the best deals.

ON HOT, hazy days, nothing refreshes the spirit quite like the sight of sparkling water— at the beach or in the backyard. An uncle of the groom owned a farm whose lawns rolled down to the borders of a placid bay, complete with bobbing dock. Separated from the shore by a small grassy strip, a stone-tiled swimming pool mirrored the deep blue of the waters beyond *(opposite)*. A patio of soothing gray-blue slate, gently fenced by a marshland of fuzzy cattails, provided the perfect stage for cocktails at our languid summer reception.

The gorgeous setting needed little embellishment, but for the occasion, Preston flanked the area with a pair of pom-pom trees fashioned from vibernum branches and smoke—*Cotinus coggyria*—a fizzy-leafed foliage. Like cotton-candy clouds, the arrangements seemed to float above the cocktail party. In shape and color, the metal stands that held the branches matched the café tables, which in turn shared the steely shade of the slate. To show off the shapely legs of the small tables, Todd skirted them in short silk squares.

The cocktail party centered around the pool, but guests were encouraged to amble along the water's edge, where teak Indonesian lounge chairs provided a peaceful vantage point from which to watch the setting sun *(right)*. A reggae group's irresistible rhythms inspired many to move—guests sambaed

barefoot in the grass, and the poolside patio made a convenient dance floor. Before dinner, a bossa nova band took over. Its jazzy melodies gently underscored the meal, and the sultry strains of Latin love songs made the moonrise that much more romantic. Both groups played additional sets after dinner.

fabric, alternated gold and green. Patchwork napkins, too, varied chevron swatches of color on the almost-set table *(opposite).* We duplicated this technique for the poolside cocktail tables.

I selected stemware tinted a deep green—a modern take on grandma's Depression glass. Gleaming lusterware—yet another retro touch—rested atop the tablecloths. Chartreuse chargers framed pearly plates and luxe linens. We tucked the menus into the napkin folds *(left).* I'd asked graphic artist Kayo der Sarkissian to condense the type into the shape of a square and to play with the point size on each line; the decidedly contemporary design had already been introduced to guests when they received their invitations. We reproduced the menu on sheets of vellum via computer, then inscribed the guests' names across the top in silver ink.

Above the bride's table, Geoff strung a ring of paper lanterns. Each vellum luminary held a single glass votive. As night fell, the candles illuminated the stretched canvas roof so that it stood out like a beacon by the shore. A perfect pyramid of minty cymbidium orchids and miniature celadon chrysanthemums pointed up past the paper chandelier to the center of the sheltering tent *(overleaf).* Smaller awnings, fringed on the edges and flagged on top, shaded the guest tables.

WE SET THE TABLES in shades that rivaled the lush green lawns and vivid blue skies of our scenic inlet. The bright, shiny silks brought to mind the fresh melons and tropical fruits of the season—honeydew, kiwi, cantaloupe, mango. Like zest of lemon, the punch of colors invigorated the senses. The bride's tablecloth, sewn from four sections of

refreshments

dressed everything from salty margaritas to tart vodka tonics to sweet Tom Collinses *(left)*. For a decorative touch, we planted a pyramid of limes on one end of the bar *(below)*.

Preston and Geoff collaborated to create the evocative tropical bar. Built around the sturdy framework of a basic rental table, columns of freshly cut bamboo formed the organic foundation. A hefty slab of Plexiglas,

S U N L I G H T   S T R E A M E D through the stained glass of champagne flutes, martini beakers, and broad tumblers arranged in rows on a bamboo bar at the foot of the pool *(opposite)*. Frosty pitchers were filled with freshly squeezed citrus extracts, infused sparkling water, or a choice of clear liquors, and each beverage was served from a container in a complementary hue—sunny yellow for rum, lime green for gin, warm amber for tequila, and cool celery for vodka. Wedges of citrus

three-quarters of an inch thick, topped the hollow stems. To fit it into my green scheme, Geoff painted the underside a vibrant shade of celadon. As night approached, we illuminated the bar from below with small spotlights. Caught up in the euphoria of the occasion, the guests figured it was moon glow that lit the luminous counter.

Waiters circulated with a choice of three hors d'oeuvres, but I also wanted a buffet for the cocktail hour, so we positioned one opposite the bar, at the other end of the pool. Peter and I playfully labeled it the fire-and-ice station, because Preston bordered the base of the ice block with poufs of pink-gray smoke foliage *(opposite)*. From a distance, the shrubbery looked like the vapor of dry ice and effectively veiled any rough, dripping edges. Incorporating the same tropical elements as the cocktail bar, the bamboo buffet station would have been equally at home on the beaches of Brazil.

The buffet hors d'oeuvres also ran hot and cold. Fiery, coal-stoked hibachis flanked the ice block, ready to grill savory stakes of squab, shrimp, and vegetarian ravioli *(top)*. Each kabob combined a number of seasonal tastes: a citrus-honey mix marinated the poultry cubes; crisp rice noodles coated the shrimp pops; and carrots, cabbage, cilantro, and shiitake stuffed the pasta pockets. Peter even used firm stems of rosemary and scallion stalks as aromatic skewers—the minty herb perfumed the meat with its distinctive fragrance *(page 99, bottom)*. In the center of the buffet, the ice

made elegant accessories—what fun to sip one nonchalantly while chatting with friends!

Todd dolled up café tables with nubby silk squares that matched the shades of the slush cocktails *(left)*. For centerpieces, broad bamboo vases held bristly cattail blossoms. To illuminate the night, I asked Geoff to plant dozens of lanterns about the lawn. Using thin wire and filament, he enclosed clear glass votives in cylinders of stiff, canary-colored vellum, and hung them from inch-wide bamboo rods. As the receding sun silhouetted the cattail spires, our amber lamps came to life, flickering along with the fireflies.

block chilled heaping platters of green shrimp *(page 96, center)* and stone crab claws—just like at Joe's, the legendary Miami hot spot. Pots of saffron sauce accompanied the cracked claws *(page 96, bottom)*, and orchid stems, preserved to order, floated in the frozen waters below.

As they arrived poolside for the cocktail party, guests were offered slush martinis in kiwi or mango *(opposite)*. Orchid blossoms and spearmint sprigs festooned the frosty drinks. Served in assorted glasses tinted soft shades of green or gold, the fruity cocktails

Summer Menu

HORS D'OEUVRES

Fire-and-Ice Hors d'Oeuvres Station

Vegetarian Wonton Ravioli Skewers

Squab Kabobs

Shrimp Pops

Iced Green Shrimp

Iced Stone Crab Claws

Butlered Hors d'Oeuvres

Lobster-Potato Petits Fours

Plaintain Chicken with Papaya

Corn Blinis with Cilantro
Crème Fraîche and Pancetta

FIRST COURSE

Chilled Plum-Lemon Heirloom
Tomato Soup with Cilantro and
Tomatillo Confetti

ENTRÉE

Grilled Red Snapper

Hash of Roasted Morning-Harvest Corn

Crimson and Gold Baby Beets

DESSERT

Grilled-Fruit Napoleon

Lemon and Pistachio Gelati

Wedding Cake

THE EVENING commenced with fruity cocktails by the pool. Guests strolling the grounds found their way to the bamboo wet bar and fire-and-ice buffet, while waiters bearing trays of savories approached those seated at the café tables or in the teak lounge chairs. We butlered three inventive hors d'oeuvres, each combining seasonal produce with distinctly Pan-American accents.

Hors d'Oeuvres

On the first circulated plate, cubes of roast potato provided a spongy square for plump lobster chunks, and a dot of avocado crowned each bite *(opposite)*. The petits fours were served on woven cucumber ribbons—an exquisitely fresh presentation. For the second, the fleshy fruit of papaya blazed yellow and pink, like a summer sunset *(page 102, top)*. A scattering of seeds peppered the sweet pulp. Orbiting this solar center, quick-seared plantain cones cocooned slices of chicken breast. Parsley leaf and papaya pieces flavored the crunchy cornets. On separate platters, florets of sage flagged miniature mounds of pancetta set in a firmament of cilantro-infused crème fraîche *(page 102, bottom)*. Disks of roasted corn bread completed the tart blinis.

As guests took their seats at the intimate dinner tables, they were greeted with

ponents mix complementary materials and styles. It takes some experimenting, but the right combination loosens up even the most formal affair by bringing a subtle sense of humor to the place setting. And at our summer reception—beside the pool, under the glow of our bamboo lanterns—casual was the order of the day, so we didn't shy away from items that had a slight hint of kitsch about them. Opalescent lusterware in pea green or squash yellow picked up the sheen of the shantung table skirts. On top of these chargers, plates gleamed a barely detectable celadon. Basic glazed crocks served as soup bowls.

bowls of chilled gazpacho. Recipes for the robust soup date back hundreds of years, and we maintained tradition by making ours from heirloom lemon tomatoes and husked green tomatillos (opposite). Peter garnished the thick broth with a cilantro-tomatillo confetti.

Entrée

Right down to the ribboned, gauze-wrapped lemon halves, we prepared the tables for an entrée of grilled fish. Personally, I think tables are most interesting when the central com-

The red snapper was as fresh as if it had just been pulled from the bay. In the luau spirit, we loaded long grills with hardwood coals and caged them in with rented grates. Peter orchestrated a trio of grill-masters as they flipped the fish, and guests delighted in the smoky spectacle. When seared to perfection, each crisp fillet of snapper was placed atop a bed of pebbly corn kernels *(above)*. Buried in the beach of roasted hash was a treasure of crimson and gold baby beets.

Summer Sorbets

For dessert, we served fruit cups—literally: scooped-out lemons and limes held dripping dollops of sweet gelato. Pistachio cream topped with nuts melted into lemon cups, while tart lemon sorbet, capped with zesty corkscrews, filled the limes. Alongside these juicy citrus balls, squares of grilled pineapple and papaya sandwiched succulent melon slices *(opposite)*. Flowering spearmint sprigs garnished the tropical napoleons.

the cake

ALTHOUGH I typically prefer three-tiered cakes, Margaret convinced me to make an exception to my rule, arguing that each of the six layers in her summer skyscraper enhanced the one beneath it, building to an elegant crescendo at its peak *(right)*. Setting the statuesque structure on the narrowest diameter I could rent, a twenty-inch round, further emphasized its height.

How to describe the magnificent monument? Each level of the tower was trimmed

in gilt braid and strung with pearls. Like punched tin, panel upon panel featured florid scrolls *(left)*. Tassels of icing hung from one tier, delicate petals from the next, and so on—up, up to the gilded dome. To achieve her subtle shades, Margaret used paintbrushes dusted with gold powder and steeped in pastel sugar glazes, then blended to her heart's content. She frosted the cake with fondant, the logical choice for summer. The smooth shell repels flies and holds up under heat. To further shelter our splendid dessert from the elements, we shaded it under a pale green parasol hung with sheer panels of gauze *(opposite)*.

ALTHOUGH THE details of a summer reception may be ordered and organized in much cooler months, think ahead to the specific demands of the season—particularly when planning an outdoor event. Seaside receptions can be wonderfully relaxing, as long as certain uncontrollable elements (sand, wind, water) are taken into consideration. For example, Geoff and I made ample use of netting and umbrellas, which sheltered diners from insects and shaded them from the sun. (Bathrooms were also stocked with sunscreen and bug repellent.) I decided to cushion the seats in fabrics that matched the tablecloths— not a standard rental option. Instead, I asked Todd to design pillowcases in the same kiwi-colored silk used for the tables. For a royal touch, he trimmed the borders with gold *(opposite)*. Advance planning cuts back on expenses as well: we paid less for the material by calculating our needs for tablecloths, napkins, and seat covers, then buying all the fabric in bulk.

The Invitation

To convey the casual style of our poolside reception, we kept the invitations contemporary—printed on vellum and folded simply into envelopes of heavy-weight paper in primary yellow *(above)*. A square of funky type announced: "Bare Feet Welcome!" Invitations should alert guests to the appropriate dress code. In our case, grassy lawns would have been inhospitable to heels. The lighthearted line about bare feet made it clear that formal attire was not required.

Tents and Lights

Tassels festooned the cheerful canvas tops that covered each of the intimate dining tables.

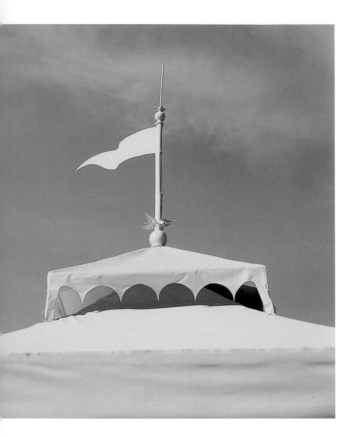

painted the same pale green of the canvas ceiling. As darkness approached, the votive candles that glowed from within each cylinder seemed to float, unassisted, in the night sky.

We decorated the lawn with other whimsical ornaments that actually served very practical purposes. In addition to an assortment of vellum lanterns, we staked playful cedar spirals on bamboo branches *(below)*. The slow-burning incense scented the air with oriental notes, and its smoky odor acted as a natural insect repellent.

Although these individual umbrellas stood on single poles of cut bamboo, the four-cornered bridal tent was custom-fit to a metal framework. After we'd unfurled the pale-green painted awning, we further distinguished it with billowing gauze panels, a scallop-edged, marigold-colored cap, and a ceremonial flag, flying at full mast *(above)*. In fact, Geoff fashioned the lemon-yellow pennant from plywood. Beneath the tent, a chandelier of paper lanterns bobbed in the breeze *(opposite)*. Geoff crafted the translucent crowns from vellum that matched the marigold of the scalloped cap, then strung them from a hoop

Exotic Orchids ❧

A few days before the marriage, while walking the lawns of the reception site, I recalled the tropical foliage that graced the oceanside gardens of a friend of mine in Marathon Key, Florida. Preston had planned the floral arrangements months before, but he agreed that my idea would make one-of-a-kind bouquets, so I called up my friend and asked him to FedEx a bunch of freshly cut sea-grape shrubbery. The package arrived the eve of the ceremony, and Preston quickly worked the broad, blue-green leaves into the bridal bouquet. They provided the perfect foil for the rest of the blossoms. Curled white tongues of exotic cymbidium orchids gleamed in contrast; compact centers of celadon chrysanthemums picked up the bluish hue; and strings of amaranth trailed over the edges *(opposite)*. Leftover leaves made charming coasters.

I admit to a fondness for monochromatic combinations that nonetheless are unique. In other words, although a complementary color scheme unifies the bouquets, they are by no means identical. I also like the shapes of the blossoms to define the line of the bouquet. Unencumbered by fussy floral fillers, the arrangements appear more natural. For the maid of honor, Preston interspersed orchids among bunches of blueberries and velvet cattails *(bottom)*. Pale as sea glass, the soft shades ranged from misty green to pebble blue and sandy buff. Another bridesmaid carried a simple, chic cluster of orchid blossoms *(top)*, fringed with pearly amaranth

others—and a few infatuated bumblebees—gazed upon small staircases of orchids and chrysanthemums, which spilled right onto the silk cloths *(left)*.

Personalized Paddle Fans

To catch the cool breeze blowing off the bay, we gave each guest a flat fan *(opposite)*. I'd found a batch of plain, split-straw paddles at an Oriental import shop; then Kayo der Sarkissian, the graphic artist who produced the invitation and menu, printed a personal message, "Good friends and a gentle breeze

strands and tied with a pewter-toned ribbon. Preston bunched the stems into six-inch-long bamboo segments. The smooth, sturdy tubes made excellent handles.

To carry the tropical theme from the chapel pews to the lawn chairs, we also used the water-resistant bamboo branches as vases and alternated the arrangements by table. Miniature palm trees, made from the fuzzy fingers of cattail reeds and centered on lusterware plates, greeted some diners *(right)*, while

GOOD FRIENDS
AND A GENTLE
BREEZE
ARE BLESSINGS
THAT MAKE OUR
HEARTS SING
MAGDALENA
& SEBASTIAN

are blessings that make our hearts sing," on sunny vellum squares. With satin ribbon we laced the thoughts between the palm strands. In the sultry summer heat, these pretty tokens were immediately put to practical use.

A Blanket of Stars

For the other three seasons, I sent the bride and groom off in a getaway vehicle that encapsulated all the elements of their reception, but our shorefront spot already felt like a resort, too idyllic to abandon just yet. Instead, I built a honeymoon bed out in the open, under the stars—but far from the sight of the area's inhabitants *(right)*. For one special night, I wanted the new couple to feel as if they were alone in the Garden of Eden, the only man and woman on the face of the earth. Bamboo stalks made primitive bedposts, from which we hung sheer panels and mosquito netting. The gauzy curtains flapped in the wind like the delicate wings of dragonflies. On top of a teak-wood frame, we created a feather bed out of thick mattresses, downy comforters, and plump pillows. At the foot of the bed, a long bowl edged with golden orchids held sweet grapes, crisp apples, and assorted passion fruits. Champagne and bottled water waited in a nearby ice bucket, ready to christen the wedding night. Crickets chirped their sweet lullaby as the waves lapped against the beach. Hypnotized by passing clouds, husband and wife drifted off to sleep, knowing that they'd wake to watch the sun rise over the water.

fine points

FLOWERS

I'm a firm believer in flower power. The fragrant seasonal messengers remind us to cherish the day, and they have been associated with wedding ceremonies since time immemorial. Ancient Romans bedecked bridal chambers with blossoms and herbs. Buddhists drape couples with leis. The Japanese scatter petals to repel evil spirits. Queen Victoria, wed with a sprig of orange blossom at her breast, defined an era of matrimonial etiquette with the gesture. Contemporary couples can incorporate flowers into many aspects of their reception. Print your invitation on petal-flecked paper, spritz enclosure tissues with the essence of a preferred bloom, and post the envelope with botanical stamps. Dress doorways with welcoming wreaths, wrap columns in lush garlands, top tables with breathtaking arrangements, and bestow

The Belle Jar: Shoots of purple pansies sprout from a tumbler of cut glass. Arranged on an argentine platter, beneath a crystal-clear garden cloche bow-tied with hyacinth buds, this simple serving of spring blossoms belongs on a buffet table. Even tiny treatments shout happy tidings when they're custom-made to charm. Look again: without the two slender stems knotted on top, this arrangement wouldn't be quite so whimsical. The jaunty satin bow adds an appealingly breezy sensibility.

a single exquisite bloom at each place setting. Freeze colorful petals in ice cubes; scatter edibles across cocktails and soups; coat perfect specimens in crystallized sugar, then adhere the glittering glories to desserts. Go a little crazy, and take your cues from nature. Each season yields its own unique bounty of blossoms. Wise brides will research market selections and strategize with a florist about three months before the big day. Decide on a few signature varieties, use them in abundance, and express your reception in the language of flowers.

In spring, a bride's thoughts turn to tender buds and precious pink blooms. Although flowering branches such as dogwood are frequently used to add height to massive arrangements, I decided to flip the scale and instead secure clipped stems in modest gilt urns *(top)*. Todd Fiscus embellished the sparse branches with blushing-bride protea, pink hydrangea heads, poppy pods, ranunculus, and a dash of wild oregano. For couples marrying between seasons, roses are the classic choice. They travel well and are available year-round. Those versed in the language of flowers know that pink and red roses speak of passion. Christopher Bassett's paean to love mixes the mighty rose with miniature New Zealand calla lilies, fragrant stock, and pittosporum *(bottom)*. To complement Dorian Webb's delicate vessel of Venetian glass, Raegen McKinney crafted a subtle but stunning globe of ostrantina blossoms *(opposite)*.

Autumn and Winter: Fall offers a wild riot of colors to warm up wedding tables. Christopher Bassett chose a verdigris tin compote—its slightly aged appearance seemed right for the season—then filled it to the brim with blazing zinnias and dahlias *(above)*. Evergreen foliage epitomizes the fresh, enduring spirit of winter *(opposite)*. Plant young juniper shrubs in galvanized tin buckets (available at any hardware store), cover topsoil by fitting moss squares around the trunk, and dress with a ribbon of silver mesh.

A deconstructed centerpiece betrays the influence of ikebana, the ancient Japanese art of flower arranging *(opposite)*. Threaded through a hole pierced in the pale green cylinder, rhododendrun dominates the ceramic vase. A loose latticework of calla lilies scaffolds the cool silk runner that dresses the escort-card table at a reception in an Asian gallery. It's essential that flowers fit the locale. Country clubs are popular party venues. Bursting from a Simon Pearce basket, a profusion of spray roses, sweet pea, forget-me-nots, euonymus, euphorbia, and ivy complement the grandeur of such exclusive sites *(top)*. Landscaping efforts unveiled a perfectly round bird's nest residing in a cedar branch *(bottom)*, so I insisted Christopher Bassett include the humble home in a summer arrangement. He asked a pastel egg to inhabit the brambles, invited a silk butterfly to visit, and scattered the tabletop with petals of tea roses.

What a gracious gesture to give each guest a colorful nosegay! A posy of muscari, lilac, pansy, and euphorbia makes a most delicate place-card rest *(top)*. Floating narcissus blossoms and euphorbia leaves transform aureate Victorian compotes into individual reflection pools that fit in the palm of the hand *(bottom)*. With tall, slender stands, wide mouths, and a variety of designs, compotes are versatile vases that command attention. For disarming centerpieces, cluster the crystal goblets in threes. Arrangements accentuate the dining room, of course, but also buffet stations, mantelpieces, and cocktail and escort-card tables *(opposite)*. Christopher Bassett created a serene floral altar by tying a clutch of well-conditioned lily of the valley to the stem of a compote with thin metallic ribbon. Golden accents travel up the container to the gilded garland circling the cup and the glittering mesh encasing the votive.

Ms. Stacy Faber

Mr. Thomas Camay

Mr. & Mrs. George Vincent

Mr. Edgar St...
Ms. Leonora Dav...

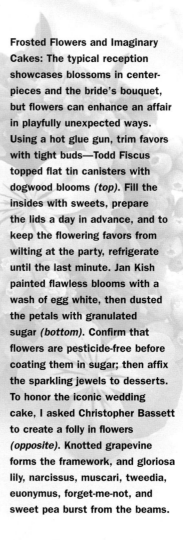

Frosted Flowers and Imaginary Cakes: The typical reception showcases blossoms in centerpieces and the bride's bouquet, but flowers can enhance an affair in playfully unexpected ways. Using a hot glue gun, trim favors with tight buds—Todd Fiscus topped flat tin canisters with dogwood blooms *(top)*. Fill the insides with sweets, prepare the lids a day in advance, and to keep the flowering favors from wilting at the party, refrigerate until the last minute. Jan Kish painted flawless blooms with a wash of egg white, then dusted the petals with granulated sugar *(bottom)*. Confirm that flowers are pesticide-free before coating them in sugar; then affix the sparkling jewels to desserts. To honor the iconic wedding cake, I asked Christopher Bassett to create a folly in flowers *(opposite)*. Knotted grapevine forms the framework, and gloriosa lily, narcissus, muscari, tweedia, euonymus, forget-me-not, and sweet pea burst from the beams.

aut

bounti

A harvest moon the color of rust casts the country-side in a glorious amber glow, and morning introduces nature in all her maturity. Through the faceted prisms of the first frost, a kaleidoscope unfolds. Grasses blend from green to gold. Trees catch fire, their leaves blazing a rainbow of reds and oranges. Earth brings forth its offerings—pumpkins, potatoes, squash—and the sweet smoke of burning

ful
COLOR

wood perfumes crisp afternoons. Brisk winds put everything in sharper focus. This is a vivid season. Memories of a fall wedding will linger long after the day has passed. Clapboard cottages, stone-walled inns, rustic farms and ranches—the weathered, sturdy shelters that pepper rural landscapes make perfect hosts for autumn receptions, but with a little imagination, any setting can capture the spirit.

autumn THE ELEMENTS

AH, AUTUMN! I adore sweater weather, when a slight chill in the air reminds us to rake the leaves, stock the larder, and stack the hearth. Fall, full of color, is a season lucky couples will savor as they exchange their "I do's." Think of it as Mother Nature's generous gift, a beautiful backdrop for the big event.

A perfect reception draws inspiration from fall's abundant harvest, earthy palette, and poignant atmosphere. The bride and groom met years ago at a tailgate feast for their alma mater's annual homecoming weekend. A sentimental twosome, they wanted to wed on the anniversary of that special day and keep the reception as casual as their first kiss. We three agreed the gathering should be held indoors and out, at a rustic barn with a roaring bonfire.

In the process of interviewing prospective vendors, I planted the seeds of this seasonal party. The mood was to be cozy, warm and welcoming; the décor organically opulent; the meal made up of comfort foods. I start feeding ideas to vendors as soon as possible. It helps me weed out those who may not be the best match for a particular event, and better yet, it allows me to benefit from the advice of those who are. Expert consultants, caterers, florists, and bakers know what questions to ask, expenses to expect, and problems to anticipate. I find that the vast majority of my preferred

vendors consider their profession their craft. The discovery of such soul mates always reassures me: It means that the person not only will consider his or her contribution an original creation, custom-designed for the event, but will also take all the other elements into account. Like the football players at that fateful homecoming game, each member of the team has to work with the others toward a common goal.

Country Comfort

Monarch butterflies and migrating geese, golden sunflower fields and happy pumpkin patches, maple leaves flickering yellow and red: the essence of autumn is most exquisitely expressed in the country. On a lazy drive to nowhere, I discovered my ideal location: a Revolutionary-era stone barn nested between grassy meadows and bordered by a maple grove. To find the farm, guests traveled beside a meandering river, over a covered bridge, past rolling hills and grazing cows. Hand-painted posts along the road pointed the way. Picturesque routes put people in the proper mood—provided that directions are clear.

A setting as spectacular as the barn begs to be unveiled at the peak of its beauty, just before twilight. A field to the side of the farm served as a discreet parking lot, and although it was easy enough for guests to park

their own cars and walk the short stretch to the barn, I suggest couples consider hiring college students to direct traffic (equip them with flashlights for after dusk) or, if the lot is more than twenty-five yards from the reception site, a valet service. For a truly authentic experience, rent several horse-drawn carriages to transport guests from the parking lot to the party. To accommodate guests, the event staff should park at the far end of the area.

Cider by the Barn

Upon arrival, each guest was offered a glass of sparkling wine or cider in a courtyard beside the barn. The setting sun kissed every leaf good-bye, and the warmth of the fading day lingered in a delightfully languid way. The only music to be heard was the whisper of wind through the trees, the murmured coos of nesting doves, and the soft lilt of conversation as guests awaited the entrance of bride and groom. This simple serenade was more relaxing than one hundred orchestrated love songs. I don't believe in bombarding the senses. Allow the afternoon to unfold naturally, in stages.

Cocktails should last at least an hour, giving guests plenty of time to get settled and greet one another. If sparkling wine is to be reserved for toasts, a full bottle will pour five glasses. If accompanying appetizers, allot one

bottle for every three guests. From the first nibble, the menu should be a well-orchestrated symphony of tastes, presented in a manner appropriate to the setting. The waiters for our country wedding were asked to wear dark shoes, black jeans, a white button-down shirt, and a white cotton apron—a look that was comfortable but smart. After offering the cider and wine, they circulated with trays of wild rice pancakes, sweet potato fries, and crunchy roasted chestnuts. I'd hand-picked an eclectic array of serving platters—vintage mirrors, collectible ceramics, wooden box trays. To show off their patterns, we made sure to frame the hors d'oeuvres with some perimeter space.

Our courtyard had a few strategically placed stone benches, and I added an assortment of wicker and wrought-iron chairs. Make sure there is sufficient seating on hand, especially for the elderly.

To announce the dinner hour, candles were sparked in the darkening barn and a jazz saxophonist began to blow his horn. Allowing for two buffet stations, a dance floor, and dining tables, our space was able to seat about seventy guests. At a sit-down dinner, I never leave placement to chance. Even intimate gatherings demand seating plans. Guests are more at ease when they don't have to make such decisions spontaneously. Station a small table with escort cards near the entrance to the cocktail area, and instruct a member of the catering crew to answer questions. As a backup, provide him or her with a clipboard listing those assigned to each table. Couples seated together can share the same card—typically a folded tent featuring names on the cover and corresponding table number inside. This enables guests to familiarize themselves with their table location at their own convenience and eliminates any confusion or crowding when it comes time to sit down. Instead of the traditional envelope and card, I asked calligrapher Lori Saucier to ink broad, burnished oak leaves in gold.

A Buffet Menu ⊂⊙⌇∾

Daniel Matrocce *(opposite, bottom)*, the caterer, advised that a buffet would best emphasize the casually elegant atmosphere I wanted to achieve for our autumn wedding. Meal-service style should be based more on mood than on money, because buffet stations, contrary to common opinion, are not necessarily more cost-effective than butlered dinners. For a relaxed environment, one that encourages guests to socialize and allows them to eat at their own pace, buffets make sense. They also work better with small groups. At large gatherings, gridlock is often the unpleasant result.

With sixty-five attendees, ours was a relatively small get-together. We set up two fully stocked serving stations, one at either end of the dining area. For most receptions, I'd esti-

mate about thirty-five people per buffet—the last thing you want is a long line of hungry, grumpy guests. Situate the stations near the dining tables, but not so close that the traffic will disturb those already seated.

Each buffet should feature the complete menu, although bigger groups and more elaborate dishes may demand several buffets and, for example, a separate carving station. To prepare guests for the tastes to come, I procured a pair of old schoolhouse chalkboards and asked Lori to write out the main-course offerings in amber-colored chalk. She also listed the wines. We propped each board atop a weathered cider barrel set against the stone walls adjacent to the buffet stations. The wait staff was also well-versed in the menu and fielded queries about ingredients.

A hodgepodge of hotel silver, hand-forged ladles, and sterling spoons, skewers, and prongs makes for offbeat serving utensils—every item on the buffet should have its own. If guests will be helping themselves, assign one server per station; otherwise, to maintain flow, allot one server to every two or three items. The crew should keep the buffets clean and orderly so that the last person on line won't miss out on the handsome display. A good caterer will replenish trays before they're completely emptied, to insure that no one is left scraping the bottom of the barrel, so to speak. And even in the case of self-service, the

More Tips for Autumn Fests

Hang a welcome wreath of golden leaves with a "Just Married" banner.

Scour flea markets for unique accessories: antique platters to pass hors d'oeuvres, vintage print handkerchiefs to use as napkins, old wedding photos that, when positioned under a glass round, make a sentimental cake table.

Hire a craftsperson to carve monograms and decorative motifs into pumpkins and squashes; illuminate them from inside with candles.

Cut a maze through a cornfield leading to the reception site.

Check the calendar, and schedule your celebration on the night of a full moon.

Cover rough or dirt courtyards and driveways with mulch or white gravel.

Press and wax fall leaves for use as coasters or place cards.

Perfect fall fabrications: jewel-toned silks, woven jacquards, gray flannel, kraft paper over gunnysack.

Bowls of gleaming green apples, miniature gourds as place-card rests, sunflower-filled vases: seasonal bounty makes beautiful decorations.

caterer should provide additional staff to assist at the dining tables—pouring wine and water, clearing plates and napkins, and attending to individual requests. Calculate at least one waiter for every fifteen guests, and heed your caterer's suggestions. The more help on hand, the smoother the service.

Stack the starting point of each station with twice as many plates as people, to accommodate those who choose to come back for seconds. But save guests the trouble of fumbling with napkins and flatware at the buffets by presetting the dining tables. For the same reason, I prefer to use great big plates, ones that permit plenty of wiggle room, so that people can fill up without fear of spilling. Nothing ruins a guest's night faster than an embarrassing food accident. Free hands, spacious plates, and preset tables help keep such minor disasters to a minimum.

Blushing Roses and Bittersweet

To convert the soaring space into a cozy cloister, I asked floral designers Katie and Michael Meeks *(page 136, top)* to fill every crook and cubbyhole with candlelight. On the tables, clay saucers hosted a harvest of beeswax apples and pears. The blush of late-blooming roses added an element of sophistication, but we kept centerpieces wide and low so that long stems wouldn't interfere with conversation.

Strands of bittersweet counterbalanced the roses' innate nobility with a touch of the wild. We gathered the berried vines into loose armloads, tied them with long organza bows, and hung the brambles along window ledges, from the base of the chalkboards, or in any empty corner. Designate at least half a day for the caterer and florist to set up. All evidence of their efforts should be out of sight—and mind—by the time guests arrive.

The Basket Cake

Baker Rosemary Littman *(page 136, center)*, celebrated for her butter-cream confections, whipped up a three-tiered masterpiece and wrapped it in basket-weave icing. The pattern, reminiscent of picnic hampers and wicker rockers, perfectly captured the essence of the country celebration. Roses from the Meekses' arrangements played the part of the muse. In the tinted sugar blossoms encircling each layer, Rosemary nearly immortalized the roses' beauty—if only the cake hadn't tasted so good!

A sweet reminder of the reason behind the reception, the wedding cake deserves to be prominently displayed. I search out unusual trays that accentuate the theme. A shabby-chic wooden bowl, turned upside down to provide support, echoed the easy charm of the cake itself. Choose a platter at least four inches wider than the cake's diameter to assure that the pièce de résistance is properly framed.

Maria's Commonsense Ideas for Courteous Hosting

As guests arrive, immediately offer a beverage—sparkling wine or water.

Don't skimp on hors d'oeuvres: calculate about eight per person during a one-hour cocktail party.

Keep bathroom kits available for guests' emergency needs.

Allow two square feet per person on the dance floor, so that half your party can be dancing comfortably at any given time. Avoid extra-large dance areas that might make guests feel self-conscious.

Later in the season, when the weather turns cool, plan for a coatroom staffed with enough help to keep check-ins and -outs moving smoothly. Offer shawls to the women in the wedding party, to avoid a mismatch of overcoats.

Double-check directions to wedding sites days before the reception. In the case of severe detours, print up a new map to distribute after the ceremony. And always opt for the scenic route.

Plan carefully: seat guests with compatible table partners.

Schedule to avoid long waits—between ceremony and reception, hors d'oeuvres and dinner, dinner and dessert.

location

A WEATHERED WOODEN signpost fringed with fiery maple leaves welcomes guests to the rustic autumnal reception *(above)*. Rough-hewn, hand-painted markers planted along the roadside serve to suggest the relaxed atmosphere of the upcoming gathering and help transport body and mind, moving family and friends from the formality of the ceremony to the comfort of the celebration. Map out the most scenic route to the reception site and include directions with the invitation. In the case of tough-to-spot turns down rural roads, I recommend creating several such signs and placing one at each troublesome intersection. Out-of-towners will thank you for your thoughtfulness.

Part of the charm of this stone barn is its seclusion. Guests were pleasantly surprised when they happened upon its open doors *(overleaf)*. Working with elements found around the farm, the Meekses fashioned an entrance so naturally festive, it looked as if it had sprouted up from the ground just in time for the occasion. To duplicate the design, loosely loop lengths of grapevine, fix them to one door, garnish with ripe Concord grapes wired together in lush clusters, and hang a handful of Moroccan lanterns in counterpoint. I scattered bales of straw to create a path and tossed mismatched oriental runners over the bedding for a colorful twist on the traditional red carpet.

With props, it's easy to create a couple of cozy alcoves in an empty barn. I pictured the cracked plaster of the aged walls in ornate, unfinished frames found through an antiques dealer *(opposite)*. An effusive bouquet of freshly clipped bittersweet branches, bundled with a gauzy ribbon and hung upside down, adds a decorative flourish without hampering the untamed spirit of the setting.

table settings

EVERY ELEMENT on the table plays a part in creating the perfect setting. Even simple arrangements—here, the dinner plates are stacked separately, at the buffet station—should look sumptuous. I like to combine assorted textures and patterns for a layered, enticingly tactile effect. For example, at our autumn reception, sleek brushed-brass forks mingled with old-fashioned wood-handled spoons *(left)*. Candlelight danced off faceted tumblers: these gold-patterned tea glasses, discovered in a Middle Eastern import shop, made an ornate yet unexpectedly casual choice for wine *(center)*. Numbered terra-cotta tiles,

glazed in burnished hues and garnished with sprigs of dried berries, directed guests to their tables *(right)*. Zelda Tanenbaum's handsome handmade-paper coasters, embossed with the pattern of a swatch of lace from the bride's grandmother's veil, doubled as place cards.

Rich shantung table skirts seeped in earthen tones of amber, cinnamon, curry, and teak glisten against chiseled stone walls and wooden roof beams. The naturally nubby fabric added another organic touch to the mix *(opposite)*. Square overlays of supple Ultrasuede topped each table, anchored by low terra-cotta vases and brass pots brimming with tendrils of

bittersweet. To make the stark, high-ceilinged space feel cozy, I hung a trio of iron chandeliers from the rafters, added ornate Moroccan lamps to the cross-beams, and rolled assorted oriental rugs over the wide wooden floorboards. Guests were seated at round tables for six, while one long, regal table was reserved for the bridal party *(right)*. Rising like a scepter from its center, a low-branched candelabrum distinguished this table just enough to indicate the importance of its occupants. And each place setting was graced with a little valentine—sage-buttermilk biscuits baked in the shape of hearts *(above)*. The overall impression was one of shelter and warmth, reminiscent of a medieval banquet or a pioneer's barn raising.

refreshments

FESTIVELY EFFERVESCENT sparkling wine bubbles with the boundless joy of a wedding celebration. Champagne, from the eponymous region of France, is the most recognizable of these elixirs, but quality sparkling wines are produced in vineyards around the world. Spanish *Cava,* German *Sekt,* and American *méthode champenoise* are just a few of the intoxicating options. For cocktails, allow one bottle for every three guests. I offered a choice of two frothy *prosecco* wines from Italy, and kept them chilled in an antique galvanized washtub stocked with ice *(opposite).*

Instead of standard serving trays, I used vintage mirrors *(left).* Scour flea markets for mirrors with decorative borders, rub a bit of gold-leaf paint over rough spots, and be sure to test the strength of the frame. To keep the glasses from sliding, I secured their bases with embossed paper coasters. Bundles of cinnamon sticks knotted with brass wire provide a fragrant flourish to the serving trays. Delicate crystal stemware adds a touch of class to fall's best brews of fresh-pressed pear and apple ciders, while retro milk bottles and cut-glass pitchers offer water and juice *(right).*

the menu

Autumn Menu

HORS D'OEUVRES

Crispy Wild Rice Pancakes with
Apple-Chipotle Chutney

Grilled Pizzas with Caramelized
Vidalia Onions, Slow-Roasted Tomatoes,
and Goat Cheese

Acorn Squash Soup with Caramelized
Chestnuts and Ginger Crème Fraîche

Roasted Chestnuts

Spicy Sweet Potato Fries

BUFFET

Grilled Marinated Breast of Pheasant
with Cranberry-Pear Compote

Dark-Meat Pheasant Pot Pie with
Curried Cream-Cheese Crust

Oven-Roasted Late Harvest Vegetables

Sweet and Sour Braised Red Cabbage

Frisée, Maytag Blue Cheese, and
Bosc Pear Salad with Sherry Vinaigrette

Buttermilk Biscuits

DESSERT

Vanilla Bean Cider
Ice Cream Sandwiches

Caramelized Pears with
Pumpkin Flan Tarts

Wedding Cake

MY FAVORITE RECEPTIONS celebrate their season, and the menu, perhaps more than any other aspect, offers an opportunity to literally taste the flavor of fall. Russet potatoes, acorn squash, carrots, chestnuts, pears—at their peak and ripe for the picking, a cornucopia of vegetables, fruits, and grains begs to be used. For inspiration, a few quick trips to the local farmer's market will prove invaluable—that's how Daniel and I started to plan our courses. To best utilize local produce, consult with your caterer to determine what's available when. At first the options may seem overwhelming, but take a deep breath. As the pungent aromas mingle with the crisp, cool autumn air, it will all start to make sense.

Hors d'Oeuvres

Compared with staged, seated table service, buffet stations or passed appetizers get guests mingling. Adjacent to our barn was a charming, stone-walled garden that seemed to exist for the sole purpose of a cocktail party. With twilight rays filtering through the trees and the faint scent of freshly cut hay lingering in the air, this verdant hamlet provided a refreshing respite after the service. Look for similar spots when scoping out potential reception sites.

There's something about fall's brisk, invigorating breezes that naturally stimulates

appetites. Guests are always famished after the ceremony, so don't keep anyone waiting for food. I like to offer at least three savory hors d'oeuvres. Wild rice pancakes topped with a dollop of apple-chipotle chutney, sprinkled with pomegranate seeds, and garnished with a sprig of rosemary *(page 150)* combine complementary textures and flavors in a single bite. Arranged on burnished wooden platters dressed with delicate, skeletal magnolia leaves, they're appealing to the eye as well, and the gleaming lacquer bowl of cheerful pomegranate seeds colorfully punctuates the presentation.

Ceramic sake cups, nestled like eggs in a bed of straw, are just the right size for individual tastings of acorn squash soup *(top)*. Nuggets of caramelized chestnuts coax out the hint of sweetness hidden in the squash, and ginger-infused crème fraîche is both soothing and slightly spicy. A bronze charger transports this rich bisque. Waxed-paper bags of roasted chestnuts were also on hand for noshing *(center)*.

We set up a long barbecue to serve one of my favorite items—grilled pizza *(opposite)*. Within minutes of lighting the coals, the air was filled with the smoky aroma of baking bread. As soon as the circles of toasting dough began to brown, they were flipped over on the grill and generously layered with savories: freshly chopped tomato sauce, vidalia onion slices, bits of smoked mozzarella or crumbled feta cheese, and portabello mushroom pieces. Cut into bite-size wedges, the pizza was passed around on old baker's baguette boards blackened with age at the edges *(bottom)*.

The Buffet

To underscore the comfortable elegance of this rustic reception, I opted for buffet service. But buffet stations need not be made from standard rental fare. I fell in love with the unique organic shapes of some freshly cut tree stumps. They lent themselves to a second life as table legs, their curves revealed by the glistening silk cloths draped across the long planks they supported. A pair of cider barrels could stand in just as nicely.

From the deep copper pot that cooked the pheasant pie to the frilled ceramic crock containing the frisée-Bosc pear salad, I freely mixed and matched platters *(opposite)*. First used to offer hors d'oeuvres, dark wooden box trays dressed up in sheets of copper foil doubled as buffet dishes. The rich crimson of sweet-and-sour braised red cabbage, splashed with ruby port and fistfuls of juniper berries, looked positively resplendent in its gilded dish. Served in a hammered copper bowl, oven-roasted root vegetables such as yams, carrots, russet potatoes, and acorn squash embodied the earth tones of the season *(top)*.

Feasting commenced with hearty grilled meats and homestyle pot pies, their robust odors wafting up to the rafters. Tangy cranberry-pear relish paired off with thick, succulent slices of marinated pheasant breast and crumbles of curried cream-cheese pie crust *(right)*. Heart-shaped buttermilk biscuits decorated the burnished copper dinner plates, spacious enough to prevent any spills.

Pears and Country Pumpkins ⟨◦⟩

Thick, textured, and slightly spicy, dessert gave a new twist to traditional autumn fare. Pears, cut into broad slices, brushed with melted sugar, and seared until golden brown, carried pumpkin tarts *(opposite)*. A spoonful of sweet cream topped the glazed, earthy custard, and granules of sugar garnished the pleasingly imperfect potter's plates. Later, after the cake was cut, waiters circulated with a variation of the classic American ice cream sandwich, one custom-concocted for the season. Daniel blended vanilla-bean ice cream with crisp apple cider, then generously served the spread on gingersnap cookies *(below)*. Between the hint of sharp cider and the heat of ginger biscuits, the sweet ice cream saucers had surprising bite. As if fallen from the farm's changing trees, leaves of white chocolate landed randomly across the platters. Guests strolled in and out of the barn, sipping mugs of hot cider and cinnamon-dusted cappucino.

the cake

FROSTED IN ENDLESSLY interwoven filaments, christened with sugared sweetheart roses and cascades of marzipan grapes, layered to the high heavens, a wedding cake is the crowning glory of any reception feast. For our country ceremony, the basket-weave design of this luscious butter-cream brought to mind the comforts of home—even the icing is tinted the warm ivory of antique lace *(opposite)*. In the spirit of the harvest, each of the three tiers overflows with a bounty of miniature marzipan fruits and pastillage flowers.

Sugar is the magical ingredient whipped, molded, piped, and painted into such fanciful shapes. Ask the baker to make extra marzipan sweets, so that each plate can be enlivened with decorative fruits *(below)*.

When a cake tastes as good as it looks, substantial slices will be much appreciated. And who could resist flavorful layers of maple-walnut sponge touched with the golden essence of pear? Subtle, nuanced, this harmonious combination drew the evening to a delicious conclusion.

A WEDDING IS LIKE a theatrical production with only one curtain call. The couple, of course, is the star of the show, but behind the scenes, the details bring it all together. Before I craft the charming touches that distinguish a reception, I begin with the big picture. I take into account everything from the couple's favorite song to the story of how they met. To get the feel of the location, I walk through it several times. At first sight, in terms of comfort, our empty, wide-open barn appeared less than accommodating, but its inherent assets soon revealed themselves. It had good "bones"—wonderful cracked-plaster walls, rustic exposed rafters, and an

enormous stone hearth. To truly come alive, all it needed was a little color, lots of candle-light, and that old "Black Magic" (the hybrid name of our burnished aubergine roses!).

A Bushel of Beeswax Apples

More than a mere token of affection, a keep-sake—especially when it's a candle—kindles memories of the gathering *(opposite and left)*. I fell in love with the sweet beeswax apples and pears we'd placed in clay bowls on the

tables, so I ordered extras, and offered one to each guest as a thank-you. Tiny totes woven from raffia transported the tender fruits.

Lighting

The proper level of lighting greatly affects the mood of a reception. A room steeped in darkness alters the atmosphere from inviting to intimidating; excessively bright spaces make guests feel exposed. We'd already strung candle-burning chandeliers from the rafters of the barn. To add to the celestial aura, we further filled the space with a galaxy of lanterns, each twinkling with the flame of a long-burning tea light.

The Invitation

Much to my delight, Esther Smith and Dikko Faust of Purgatory Pie Press uncovered a rare set of wooden type. More than any elaborate engraving, this simple, century-old letterpress font made perfect sense for our country wedding. We selected a rough, recycled paper that looked like a piece of weathered barn wall seeped in soft plum paint, coated the wooden blocks in warm auburn ink, and printed the invitation, map, and RSVP postcard *(page 161, top)*. A square featuring a grapevine insignia sealed the heathered, off-white envelope.

Garden Roses

Hardy and easy to handle, cut garden roses can last for days in water. When it comes to casual decorating, their appeal is equal parts practicality and prettiness. To soak the barn in deep,

seasonal hues, we selected lush, late-harvest blooms. Black Magic and bright, pumpkin-colored roses burst like embers from the smoldering silk tablecloths. I asked the Meekses to create two oversize centerpieces (one for each buffet station) and three or four smaller arrangements per table. For the center-pieces, we grouped similar shades together and let the blossoms spill over the edges of the pedestal urn. A gilt frame encircled the base, and within its borders we piled succulent Bosc pears *(page 163, top)*. Clusters of the same flowers, tucked into terra-cotta pots, echoed the theme throughout the dining room.

The Great Escape ☙

The rose also claimed pride of place in the bosom of the bridal bouquet, crowning the berrylike rose hips in an old-fashioned, Biedermeier-style arrangement *(page 162)*. For the bridesmaids, a less formal take breaks up the condensed concentric circles into loose groupings of calla lilies, rose hips, and roses *(page 163, bottom)*. I recommend that every bride order two bouquets—one to have and hold, the other to toss to the girls before heading off on the honeymoon. And what better way to hit the road than in a getaway car strung with country brambles? Maple branches entwined with bittersweet trailed behind a shiny bumper *(right)*, and a piece of old barn wood gussied itself up for the occa-sion. Colorful terra-cotta letters affixed to the plank with a hot glue gun announced the happy news: "Just Married." ☙

CONFECTIONS

How sweet it is to wed—maybe that's why the tradition of offering an elaborate, one-of-a-kind cake has endured for centuries. At most receptions, the ritual of cake-cutting is second only to the first kiss in crowd-pleasing popularity. When bride and groom break the icing and slice into the symbolic confection together, they confirm their shared commitment to savor whatever life may bring.

Chances are, your parents served a classic butter-cream after their ceremony. The tiered ivory tower is still an elegant option, but couples today can choose from many other alternatives. A wedding cake, whatever its style, should be an exuberant expression, so don't be shy! Ask friends for referrals. Other vendors, such as florists and caterers, will be able to make suggestions based on their past experience. Provided you

Treat guests to their very own wedding cake. Shortbread cookies frosted with royal icing make tasty favors. Confectionary-supply sources stock everything you'll need, including recipes, but why not hire an expert? It takes practice to wield a pastry bag with the same level of finesse as a wedding cake specialist like Gail Watson. She expertly decorated these goodies, then tied them with organza ribbons. Wrap take-home edibles in cellophane, glassine pouches, or origami boxes.

cover the expense, many bakers are willing to travel to your destination. But visit local bakeries, review portfolios, sample goods (my favorite task), and discuss costs. Do your homework early. The best bakers are in constant demand, and can commit their kitchens to producing only a certain number of cakes each day.

Although I can't imagine a reception without the scrumptious conclusion of a cake, I encourage including other sweets in your menu: cookies, edible flowers, petits fours. Culinary artists can create the most marvelous treats out of sugar.

Cute as a Button: At a bridesmaid's tea, sugar-coated cookies by Patti Page announced the approaching day of dress-up *(above)*. Although the biscuits were too rich to resist, friends held onto the embroidered keepsake hankies. For a February wedding, I asked the caterer to serve small bowls of frosted valentines just before pouring the coffee *(opposite)*. Platters of pretty cookies—these beauts are by Rosie's Creations—decorate dessert buffets, cake plates, teacup saucers. For tiny bites, they make a big impact.

Frosted sugar cubes are absolutely frivolous, but I can't think of a better time to serve them than at a wedding feast. Shimmering cubes piped with initials and patterns in edible silver, by Rosie's Creations, seem almost too pretty to plunk into coffee *(top)*. Jan Kish takes the sugar frenzy one step further *(bottom)*: even her bowl could be eaten! Individually molded leaves of sweet gum paste glued together with royal icing offer a bouquet of blushing rosebud squares. For a formal spring affair, I filled a gilded porcelain tray with traditional Japanese treats, then topped it with an ornate saucer that supported a filigree-footed vase containing sweet pea and rose blossoms *(opposite)*. When designing a menu, it gives me great satisfaction to include selections that reflect the couple's heritage. Visit specialty grocers and explore ethnic cookbooks for ideas to share with your caterer, or buy ready-to-serve sweets.

He loves me, he loves me not: by the wedding day, it's official, but that doesn't change the charm of a daisy *(opposite)*. Cheerful petits fours are sure to provoke a smile. Just like their multitiered cousins, these tiny, fillingless cakes can be decorated in a variety of styles. For a spring celebration, rose-buds adorn bridal-white fondant banded at the base with a matching pink-fondant ribbon *(top)*. Modernists in any season will appreciate the offbeat, deliciously deviant pairing of ribbed purple fondant and chartreuse, capped with a lavender pompon *(bottom)*. Cheryl Kleinman created all three versions of the delicate bites. Even when serving the cake, it's appropriate to offer additional desserts such as petits fours. Nontraditionalists on a budget may opt to forego a full meal altogether and host a champagne-and-sweets-only affair. Maximize the festivities by serving more than one type of sparkling wine.

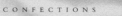

A sprinkle of whimsy, a splash of exquisiteness, and heaping dollops of delectability—that's the recipe for a great wedding cake. With the right baker, anything is possible. Polly Schoonmaker, known for her Alice-in-Wonderland aesthetic, presented me with a fun alternative to the ordinary slice of cake *(above)*. Gail Watson, aware that every bride feels like a princess on her wedding day, married gilded swirls of royal icing to snow-white fondant, then crowned the concoction with silver dragées and a string of fondant pearls *(opposite)*.

A cake is a cake is a cake: layers of baked batter frosted in sweet icing. Yet no two wedding cakes are the same. Make yours a work of art, and display it prominently on a well-dressed table—remember, the paparazzi will record it all for posterity. Jan Kish's gorgeous fondant jewel box in Wedgwood blue brims with sugared blooms *(opposite)*. Embellished with white royal icing, banded in gold like its accompanying oval platter, the exquisite creation serves as a centerpiece on dining tables. Less precious, but equally engaging, Ellen Baumwoll's kitschy cake piles fistfuls of pastel candy hearts on top of white-chocolate tiers crimped like grandma's piecrusts *(top)*. Polly Schoonmaker's pink-and-white patchwork sits like a stack of hatboxes on a country-gingham tablecloth by Todd Moore *(bottom)*. A silk flower from a vintage straw bonnet mimics the rambling rosebuds that climb the fondant cake.

177

Fabulous Fakes: Given the choice of bona fide organic blooms or sugar counterfeits, I always opt for the botanical forgeries when decorating a cake. For me, it's a matter of logic: a wedding cake ought to be completely consumable—up, down, inside, and out. Many flowers, alas, are not. It can be difficult to confirm that cut blooms are pesticide-free, and bakers can duplicate Mother Nature's handiwork with such astonishing precision, even the most discriminating gardeners would approve. It's hard to believe the roses, sweet peas, and pale violets spilling down the side of Gail Watson's tiered fondant cake are made of sugar, not porcelain *(top)*. Above embossed fondant belts tinted like antique photographs, Ellen Baumwoll planted a posy of roses *(bottom)*. For a surrealist tableau, Gail Watson baked tens of tiny wedding cakes, and I stacked them in the traditional tiered shape on three to-order graduated plate-glass disks *(opposite)*.

Most bakers deliver their goods on chipboard rounds wrapped in fabric or foil, but I'm always on the lookout for fresh ways to present wedding cakes. In my quest, I've experimented with sterling trays, breadboards, sheet metals—and one lucky birdbath. Recently, I found a papermaker who crafts deckle-edged rounds that make excellent place mats. Artists use the same weight of paper for painting. To execute the softly torn edge, the paper must be ripped when it's still a bit wet. Christopher Bassett decorated the pleasingly imperfect shape with confetti diamonds, and Polly Schoonmaker contributed a smooth, mocha-colored cake *(opposite)*. To flatter a more formal confection, calligrapher Stephannie Barba penned a monogram in gold ink *(bottom)*. Another option, versatile plate glass, can be sandblasted with monograms and decorative motifs, such as Stephannie's furled bow and flowers *(top)*.

Something Blue: For a memorable cake, the surest means of success is to select a baker whose designs make your heart sing. Choose carefully. The partnership you forge is charged with the awesome responsibility of translating your most personal ideas into a deliciously tangible form. And be open to inspiration—from something old, such as antique bride-and-groom cake-toppers *(above)*, or something new, like Margaret Braun's periwinkle pyramid *(opposite)*. Who could ever forget a blue wedding cake?

celebra
IN TH

Winter's stormy weather turns the world into a glistening wonderland. Bedecked with icicle jewels, even the bleakest terrains dress up for the arrival of a new year. Like the ancients, we herald yuletide, gathering our loved ones together to enact our own rituals against the tempest. From the flame of a candle to the blaze of a fire, we spark our own light when the days are shortest and welcome the slow return of the sun.

ting SNOW

When I think of winter, I think of the gentle hush of falling snow, the graceful silhouettes of bare branches in sleepy woods. I think of family and friends under one roof, safe and sound. Winter is a time to give thanks. So huddle a little closer for warmth. Write your names together in the snow. Make a wish out loud, and watch it crystallize into a frosted whisper. Marry in this most magical season.

winter

THE ELEMENTS

MENTION THE WORDS "winter wedding," and many couples reach for the phone to call their travel agent and book a flight to some sultry isle where they can exchange "I do's" in tropical temperatures. Fight that impulse, and think twice about the benefits of blustery nuptials. Winter is the season of celebrations: the solstice, sacred holidays, the new year, even the feast of St. Valentine. Why not choose it to christen your new life together? My imagination thrills to thoughts of cozy rooms, crackling hearths, and satin gowns. Gold, silver, and crystal sparkle all the more when set against a backdrop of snowdrifts. Brides and grooms concerned about the bottom line will also be relieved to learn that most locations offer discounts during the so-called off-season because they are less heavily booked (that is, of course, on non-holiday weekends).

Ski Chalets and Clapboard Chapels

Ski lodges, clapboard bed-and-breakfasts, chalets and castles, townhouses, ballrooms with grand fireplaces: all possess the two ingredients essential for a magical winter wedding—namely, they're warm on the inside but scenic in the snow. My January reverie brought me home to New England where, to commemorate twenty years of marriage, friends of mine planned to renew their vows *(opposite, center)*. Their first wedding had been a simple civil ceremony, and they both felt that, after two decades together, a proper celebration was both long overdue and well-deserved. I suggested a twilight service at the classic clapboard chapel, designed by Stanford White, that sits atop a hill in their tiny hamlet. Afterward, guests were invited back to a family house for dinner.

In winter, on the cusp of a new year, a marriage at home before family members and old friends brings another generational cycle full circle. Walls resonate with the memory of merry holidays, and every room echoes with personal history. The atmosphere couldn't be more intimate. I cherish the day of my own small wedding in my parents' backyard, and recommend—with careful caveats—home ceremonies to those who have both the space to accommodate guests and the sheer strength to welcome so many over their threshold.

Colder climes require that you do indeed open the doors—guests won't be lingering in the garden but rather tramping up the walk, stamping out the snow on their boots, and shaking the wet flakes from their many wrappings.

Happily, for this winter reception, the couple had access to a handsome clapboard colonial owned by cousins. Couched in the Connecticut mountains, where the word "charming" may have been coined, it provided the perfect setting for a snow-covered wedding celebration. I suggested we keep the guest list to a minimum, and indulge in a truly formal fête. One of the very first things we did was designate an official coatroom, then "waterproof" it with old rugs and big buckets for dripping umbrellas and boots.

In any season, home receptions take an emotional and physical toll on all involved. I know from my own experience. The furniture must be rearranged or temporarily removed. Common household clutter must be hidden away, and the entire place cleaned. Privacy is a precious commodity. For days leading up to the event, vendors will be traipsing in and out, and then there's the wear and tear of traffic, both pedestrian and automotive, on the property. Winter brings the added bonus of driveways to shovel and sidewalks to mulch. In the middle of this commotion, bride, groom, and members of the wedding party must dress and otherwise prepare themselves. The entire experience can be both challenging and rewarding, so I insist that couples think through the demands before making any decisions.

An Intimate Gathering ✂

We limited the guest list to forty, inviting close relatives, dear friends—and Kotzebue, the family dog *(page 187, top)*, who, for the occasion, wore a collar of chunky pearls threaded on a silk cord by the couple's daughters *(page 187, bottom)*. The small size of the party, combined with the savings afforded by holding the reception at home, allowed us to pull out all the stops.

Upon arrival, guests were ushered in from the cold to our coatroom—actually the library, just off the entrance hallway and conveniently close to a powder room. Three rolling racks with plenty of heavy cedar hangers stood in front of the bookshelves, and a well-worn oriental runner covered half the floor space, waiting for wet boots. A long oak table collected bags and packages, while a handsome old crock, once used to hold flour, now served as an umbrella repository. A roaring fireplace warmed the room, instantly melting any memories of the chilly weather. Although the caterer suggested an extra staff person to check coats, we hired a neighbor's college-age daughter, and asked her to dress like the rest of the official wait crew, in a black skirt and white blouse. She came by early to help set up the study and stock the bathrooms with necessities.

For flow, we opened the rooms, encouraging guests to mingle and permitting the caterers to quickly pass from kitchen to cocktail areas to dining hall. Days before, we'd rented a truck and loaded it up with the home's many tables, chairs, and couches, but we kept a dozen upholstered fauteuils and assorted side tables inside, and arranged them into small lounge spots throughout the two reception areas where guests gathered before supper was served.

In the gloaming, only candles lit the rooms. We placed them absolutely everywhere. Elegant lavender tapers lined the dining room table. Votives floated in wine glasses arranged along the window ledges. Outside, secured in the stiff snow drifts, tiny punched-tin lanterns illuminated the way up the drive. Long-burning candles, their flames filtering through star-shaped cutouts, cast a welcome glow.

The Single-Color Concept ❧

When it comes to designing a reception, the color scheme is a crucial factor. Sometimes a season may merit the use of many rainbow shades, but winter, in my opinion, is all about the simple impact of a few choice hues. Number one on the list? White. From ivory bridal gowns to glittering engagement rings, it really needs no explanation. Besides its association with all things traditional, white is also an incredibly contemporary color. By subtly enhancing, but never over-whelming, a space, it perfectly complements today's streamlined interiors.

At our winter reception, to blur the line between indoors and out, white reigned supreme—coloring not only the cake but the rest of the food, the favors, and the flowers as well. I asked florist Priscilla Schaefer, of Glorimundi *(opposite, bottom),* to create mono-chromatic arrangements in every imaginable shade of white. Clusters of lily of the valley, hyacinth, lisianthus, sweet pea, and Bianca rose, set in silver chalices and crystal vases, seemed to beam in the low light. Throughout the house, we camouflaged empty corners with painted brambles, and to punctuate the floral purity, we added a few invigorating bursts of green. Elegant eucalyptus stems stretched up to the ceiling in the sitting room, waxy smilax vines graced the favor table, and gleaming camellia leaves spilled out of two snow-packed silver ice-buckets flanking the front porch.

When the weather is wintry, valet service helps safely deliver loved ones right to your doorstep, and a large outdoor mat cuts down on dirty footprints inside the house. Shovel the walkways of ice and snow, but as a courtesy to guests' dress shoes, avoid using salt. Opt instead for white-pine mulch, which will absorb the wetness and give some grip to slippery surfaces without damaging leathers, suedes, and other fabrics.

Champagne and Hot Chocolate ❧

Free from the woolly cocoon of their coats, guests were welcomed into the cozy cocktail areas. A pianist played standards by Cole Porter and Nat King Cole on the family grand as waiters proffered argentine platters of hot chocolate, chilled vodka, and champagne. Savory amuse-bouches, such as brie croustade beaded with caviar and foie gras slathered across apple crisps, awakened the palate. When the clock struck six, the doors to the sunporch opened, and the beckoning fingers of a hundred candle flames drew guests into the windowed room, where the pièce de resistance, a sugar-coated ice palace by baker Toba Garrett *(page 190, center)*, held court. Because the size of the party was so small, the catering staff escorted each guest to his or her seat. Snowflake-patterned menus doubled as place cards and detailed the five-course meal to come. Chandelier crystals strung from the ceiling caught the last rays of sunlight, and the delicate framework of classic white ballroom chairs mimicked the rows of icicles hanging from the window ledges outside.

Hiring Help ❧

Even if the number of people attending the reception appears manageable, couples absolutely must hire help for a home wedding. Parents and siblings should not be stuck slaving in the kitchen and clearing plates! A marriage is a family affair, so they, too, deserve to enjoy the day. For the butlered dinner, our caterer, Great Performances *(page 190, top)*, recommended two waiters for every ten guests. In addition, another two waiters tended to the children; two bartenders prepared drinks; chef John Reilly, sous-chef Rachel John, and pastry chef Newton Pryce manned the kitchen; and a maître d' supervised the entire staff. One mark of a truly formal affair is the seamlessness with which it is executed. With the aid of a sufficiently large catering crew, every need can be met immediately and with the utmost discretion.

The Children's Room

To include children in the festivities without stifling their energy, we gave them their own room. Their round dining table was dressed with the same cotton undercloth used for the grown-ups but was topped with a large sheet of white butcher paper. A silver mug filled with crayons for doodling sat at each place setting (the bride and groom even saved some of the cute drawings for their album). We dispensed with the sophisticated menu of lobster and veal, opting instead for kid-pleasing pasta and mini-pizzas—always a hit. A baby-sitter kept watch over the flock and supervised the older children as they toasted marshmallows by the fireplace.

Maria's Safeguards for Sane Home Weddings

Employ a cleaning crew before and after the wedding.

Allow about eight square feet per person for a comfortable seated dinner.

Check septic systems, and stock up on extra fuses and cleaning supplies.

Have numbers on hand for guests who may need to take a taxi home.

Set aside a private room for the bride and groom.

Designate a separate space for vendors to store their coats and bags. Earmark a bathroom for the crew. Be prepared to feed anyone who works more than four hours.

Install dimmers for atmospheric light.

Plan for rentals to arrive the day before the wedding, tents at least two days in advance.

Drafts cause candles to burn quickly: test burning times in actual locales and account for extras.

Alert neighborhood authorities of party plans; for large receptions, hire discreet security.

location

A HOME WEDDING in winter: frost paints every window pane. Outside, white shoulders of snow, glistening with diamond dust, snuggle up to the entrance of your private crystal palace. A strand of tin lanterns encircles the estate. Small flames, safe from the wind behind walls of glass, dissolve the encroaching ice with warmth. At the gate, two sterling urns spill over with evergreen branches, their gleaming leaves punctuating the blank canvas.

To create this charming scene, we began by lining the pathways with punched-tin lanterns *(right)*. Months before, in the

planning stages, we'd scoped out three key spots. When the morning of the magical day arrived, we returned to these junctures with a small truckload of lanterns, situating several dozen along the rails of an old wooden bridge, up the walk to the entrance, and at the final turn of the drive, where we flagged each one with a pennant *(page 194)*. Cut from starched cotton and stenciled in silver paint with the family monogram, these triangles of fabric were pinned to thin bamboo stakes (I'd found a bunch at a garden supply store and sprayed the lot silver). More lanterns shone like beacons along the balustrade and winked from every window. About a half-hour before guests were due to arrive, we sparked them all with six-inch butane torches. Compact and quick, this handy tool saves time when you've got hundreds of candles to light.

For a special flourish, I asked Priscilla to fashion a pair of finials for the front gate *(opposite and below)*. We recruited a set of silver ice buckets and, working the season to our advantage, packed each one with snow, then stuffed both with branches of glossy, deep green camellia leaves.

table settings

ALTHOUGH I wanted the winter reception to be quite formal, I never lost sight of the fact that this was the family home. To extend the welcome from the front door to the dining room, I decided to seat all forty guests at one long table *(opposite)*. A single-table seating arrangement is simple to achieve with a smaller party, and it instantly establishes a sense of intimacy among the guests.

To fit the space, I reconfigured three rectangular rental tables into a U shape. In keeping with the white-on-white winter theme, tables were first draped with square cotton undercloths, then covered with rentable cotton quilts. These layers of fabrics served several purposes. They effectively covered up the rental tables, which often have rough, unfinished surfaces. They cushioned the setting, providing a soft bed for the silverware, candlesticks, and plates. And from a purely aesthetic point of view, the quilted cotton conveyed a feeling of warmth, as if the entire reception were bundled up in soft, downy blankets. Seated on scrolled thrones of white wrought iron, bride and groom took their rightful place in the center of the U.

With walls of windows worthy of Versailles, the room was flooded with light. To

evoke the fantasy of floating inside a cloud, I strung chandelier crystals along the glass panes so that their facets could catch the sun and filter it in delicate rays across the space. A pair of antique silver-filigreed lampshades atop crystal candlesticks flanked the bride and groom's place settings *(page 198, right)*. Low rows of votives, teamed with elegant lavender tapers, lined the tables. Just this side of white, lavender proved the perfect shade to accent the snowy landscape. Discounting the green of the side-table centerpieces, it was the only other color I used, and I used it sparingly— in the soft silk-screen wash of the snowflake-patterned menu *(page 198, left)* and the thin columns of candles. As dusk approached, flames alone illuminated the room.

At each setting, porcelain finger bowls bowed to old-world formality *(page 198, center)*. Tender white florets floated on the surface of each saucer's little lake. Fastened with the silver skeleton of a magnolia leaf, napkins sat aside, ready to dry fingertips.

Over the course of many trips to Mexico, the couple had accumulated an impressive assortment of sterling silver chalices—some old, some new. I scattered these small urns, filled with fresh white flowers, along the length of the table. In the center of the U, a small circular pedestal supported a crystal compote that spilled forth smilax vines *(opposite)*. The arrangement helped fill the void in the middle of the room, and it attracted attention to the molded-sugar boxes each guest would take away as a favor.

refreshments

UPON ENTERING the salon, guests were presented with a choice of aperitifs—chilled vodkas, champagne, or hot chocolate—all guaranteed to start a fire in the belly. The vodka, a sharp chaser for the caviar and foie gras hors d'oeuvres, sat in short portions in streamlined crystal shot glasses *(left)*. Secured by a silver-edged linen, the clear cylinders were proffered atop a glass cake plate. *Chocolat chaud*, served au naturel or spiked with liqueur, filled fluted tumblers, its rich umber peeking through their whimsical patterns *(center)*. An ornately trimmed silver tray played opposite the cups' droll charm, while steaming silver pots stood by, ready for seconds *(right)*. At the end of the meal, these pitchers were back in business for coffee and tea service. We offered champagne indoors *(opposite)* and out. Buffed for the occasion, galvanized buckets filled with snow chilled the sparkling wine for those brave souls who ventured onto the porch to puff a cigar or stare at the stars *(overleaf)*.

To simplify table service, limit butlered beverages to a few selections that reinforce the theme of your reception, but to splurge do stock a complete bar as well. Guests particular about their liquor will thank you for it.

Winter Menu

HORS D'OEUVRES

Brie Croustade with Caviar
and Crème Fraîche

Foie Gras and Green Apple Slivers
on Baked-Apple Crisps

APPETIZER

Napoleon of Sea Scallops
and Black Truffles

FIRST COURSE

Lobster Risotto

INTERMEZZO

Kiwi and Lime Granita

ENTRÉE

Veal Chop with a
Zinfandel Reduction

Braised Escarole and Fennel

Seared Cipolini Onions

Roasted Red Peppers stuffed
with White Bean Flan

DESSERT

Warm Vanilla Soufflé with
Vanilla-Bean Sauce

Meringue and
Vanilla Creme Cones

Wedding Cake

WINTER'S CHILL calls for hearty foods that will warm body and soul. The challenge is to create a satisfying menu that won't leave guests too stuffed to waltz between courses. From hors d'oeuvres through dessert, a solid dinner pairs seasonal produce with wines that enhance its tastes. Each course builds on, but never repeats, the flavors of the one before it. Moreover, I wanted the winter meal to mirror the elegant, all-white wedding scheme not only in its culinary refinement but also in its visual presentation. Appearance does count.

In keeping with the formal atmosphere, the dinner was to be butlered. Each course would be served to each individual guest from the left and later removed from the right. Two waiters per ten guests insures smooth trafficking of plates. Taking into consideration the small size of the gathering, I opted for rather rarefied dishes and admittedly took liberties with the menu. It's unusual, if not absolutely unlikely, to offer such items as risotto or soufflé to more than fifty guests. What can easily be executed for twenty doesn't necessarily translate for two hundred, so rely on the chef's advice when deciding on courses. Exotic, elaborately prepared dishes will quickly lose their appeal if guests are kept waiting for them. Forego

foods too complicated to cook under normal conditions.

Although all plates were arranged in the kitchen by John and then delivered to the table by the wait staff, a separate service station occupied one corner of the dining room *(page 206)*. Conveniently, it offered extra glasses, flatware, cake plates, and—just in time for dessert—gleaming pots of tea and coffee.

Hors d'Oeuvres

For a cocktail party scheduled to last about forty-five minutes, I typically calculate eight hors d'oeuvres per person, but when in doubt, more is more. It's equally important to hire enough help to keep the food moving. For our party of forty, two waiters rotated with trays of nibbles, two circulated with cocktails, a maître d' attended to individual requests, and a bartender manned his post. All were attired in pleated black trousers, smart black ties, and spotless white shirts and jackets.

The best hors d'oeuvres are little bites, easy to eat in a single mouthful; a bit savory, in anticipation of dinner; and always delicious. For our formal reception, each one had to be more exquisite than the last. To begin with, crunchy baked-apple crisps sandwiched juicy, julienned green apples, whose slight tartness seeped into thick slices of seared foie gras *(top)*. Flowering thyme sprigs dressed the serving tray. Next up, flaky croustades flavored with brie cosseted spoonfuls of crème fraîche *(bottom)*. Glistening black beads of caviar stood out like coal eyes on a

Years ago, bride and groom were engaged over a lobster dinner. To commemorate that moment, John proposed a first course of risotto featuring the clawed crustacean. The lobster shell, propped up on one side of the plate, added to the dramatic presentation *(below)*. Pearly grains of rice dusted with chives dissolved like snowflakes on the tongue.

Diners of a bygone age benefited from the refreshing effect of a palate-cleansing course *(left)*. Honoring this tradition, Newton

snowman. Buffed to a high shine, the sterling platters reflected the crooks and crumbles of each pastry pouf.

Intermezzo and Entrée

The repast commenced with a statuesque napoleon of sea scallops, wedged with black truffle bits and stacked on crispy pancakes of threaded potatoes. A lock of bull's leaf lettuce topped the teetering tower, while segments of blood orange sat at its base. Basil olive oil flavored the plate *(page 209)*.

while grilled red peppers—skinned, seeded, and stuffed with a white bean flan—brightened up the plate. To appease root lovers, it would be simple to replace the flan with an equally creamy filling of mashed potatoes. A succulent zinfandel reduction sauce was poured over the hot plate right before rushing it to its designated diner. Seared cipolini onions basked in the juices *(page 211)*.

Cookies and Cream

As soon as the dinner plates had been cleared, coffee was offered. As a teaser of things to come, star-shaped cookies, frosted with what must have been moon dust, landed across the table in small saucers. Meringue, whipped into stiff blossoms, cupped sweet vanilla cream. A meteor shower of miniature silver dragées decorated the surface *(opppsite)*.

The unbearable lightness of a soufflé can only be achieved by true culinary artists. Because the reception was small, and the oven just right, Newton agreed to undertake the arduous task of taming this temperamental delicacy. From out of his kitchen, Cupid had sent us the perfect metal soufflé cups, complete with heart-shaped handles. The heft of the small containers kept the airy sponge cakes from floating off the plates after they'd been baked. Gently browned tuiles decorated the dishes. Served piping hot with a heaping spoonful of vanilla-bean sauce and a sifting of confectioners sugar, each soufflé billowed over the brim of its cup *(above)*. True love never tasted so sweet.

concocted a tangy intermezzo of kiwi and lime granita. Reminiscent of the new-fallen snow fringing the windows, floes of the frosted granules slowly melted into clear-cast sugar bowls. Like frozen lakes, tiny silver trays supported the individual servings. The overall effect was icy and opaque.

To counterbalance the preceding seafood with a red meat that felt whiter and lighter than other beef options, we roasted thick cuts of veal chop for the entrée. Braised escarole and fennel bedded the chops, perfuming them with their distinctive aromas,

the cake

To finish the winter fantasy, I asked Toba to top the snow-white castle with crystalline accents. She blew bubbles of sugar and let the opalescent orbs alight on a base of fondant leaves and berries. Fragile, but tempered to an icy resiliency, each bauble caught the light shining from behind it *(left)*. Embroidered organza draped the cake table, and an elaborate sterling square grounded the architectural ganache.

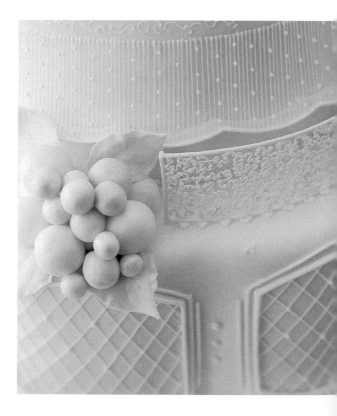

TWO TIERS OF white pound cake layered with white chocolate mousse formed the luscious interior around which Toba built her frosted mansion *(opposite)*. Using royal icing, she cast both stories in a seamless sheet of sugar. Latticework panels framed by borders of beading encircled the lower half of the cake, while an indescribably delicate fringe, woven with filaments as fine as silk and dotted with sweet droplets, skirted the upper level. A lace balcony of breathtaking intricacy stood between the two *(right)*.

SMALL WEDDINGS, especially when held at home, allow couples to indulge—after all, a budget goes further when it's covering fewer heads. If your reception will number under fifty guests, spend some of the surplus on such details as favors and flowers. After the dinner is over and the dancing done, these more palpable items are the ones that will be preserved: the invitation framed, the petals from your bouquet pressed between the pages of a keepsake book.

The Invitation

Traditionalists know that a proper invitation requires a prompt response in writing, and if your reception party consists primarily of family members and close friends, you should expect one. However, when wedding in winter, a season scheduled with holiday commitments and their corresponding travel demands, it's wise to send a "save the date" announcement six months in advance.

For our formal reception, I wanted the stationery to capture the pure, pale colors and fairy tale shapes that symbolize winter. The invitation, a folded card of the faintest ivory, featured a solitary snowflake, silkscreened in a soft plum wash within the frame of an embossed square *(opposite)*. Desgined by Heather Arak and Nathan Kanofsky, the same pattern would later greet guests at the table from the menu cover. Calligrapher Anna Pinto inscribed each envelope in a deep purple ink that echoed the tint of the snowflake motif, and an RSVP card encouraged an affirmative reply. Anna also personalized each menu so that it could double as a place card.

Lavender Tallows ✑

Hidden behind hills of snow, in the shadow of a pine forest, the family house seemed almost as secluded as the North Pole. But indoors, each room bustled with activity worthy of Santa's workshop. Roaring fireplaces welcomed guests with their warmth. We stoked the hearths with aged birch from the surrounding woods and stockpiled timber to keep the blazes burning. In casings of silver-paper bark, their curled shavings scattered on the floor below, even the logs complied with the all-white décor. For the occasion, we converted mantels into makeshift altars, covering every square inch of surface space with ceremonial candles in clear glass votives *(left)*.

Separated from the snow by little more than a wall of arched windows, the dining room acted as a looking glass onto the landscape. To further dissolve the distinction between inside and out, I filled the house with candles, scattering them about the foyer, cocktail area, even the bathrooms. In a single line along the dining room's window ledge, extra wineglasses housing twinkling tea lights acted as substitute votives. We kept boxes of extra tallows on hand in case of quick meltdowns in drafty spots. Candelabra in crystal or whitewashed wrought iron reached their arms up toward the ceiling, while strands of chandelier teardrops dappled rays across the tables. As daylight faded into dusk, the dining room transformed into a private aurora borealis, aglow with the flicker of a hundred flames *(opposite)*.

Sugared Almonds ✑

Almonds represent fertility and hope. Dipped in silvered sugar, these *bonbonbieri*—"sweet somethings," in the passionate tongue of the Italians—promise intense moments of pleasure. To contain the potent pralines, I commissioned a series of molded sugar cylinders from baker Gail Watson, each capped with flat fondant lids. Swirls, stripes, and dots of icing, occasionally trimmed in sparkling tinsel, adorned the tops, and silky ribbons wrapped up the entire package *(page 217)*.

Bridal-White Blossoms ✑

In cheerful defiance of nature's sleepy season, fresh flowers filled the house. The mono-chromatic color scheme of bridal white made a modern formal statement, and the effect was further enhanced by grouping the blooms by type. Clusters of lily of the valley, sweet pea, lisianthus, and rose spilled forth from silver chalices *(left)*. Since the ceilings were rather low—about nine feet high—correspondingly low arrangements helped the dining hall feel more open. At the same time, their smallness added to the intimacy of the gathering. Complicated arrangements would have conflicted with the intended coziness of the single-table seating. I didn't want fussy; I wanted clean, contemporary. Running in a row down the long table, the shining chalices picked up on the silverware of the place settings, while the milky blos-soms blended well with the quilted cotton tablecloths. Even the bride's bouquet echoed these themes. Barely bigger than a nosegay, tied together with a scrap of silver organza, grape hyacinth spikes, lilting lilac spires, and open anemone cups combined in a win-some ivory assemblage suitable for a winter princess *(opposite)*.

For a complementary jolt of color, I asked Priscilla to create a few simple, yet strong, arrangements in solid green. Amassing one type of plant easily accomplishes this aim. Graphically, green and white mix well—after all, the colors occur together in nature. We bunched branches of smilax, a twining brier

often used for garlands and as filler by florists, into glass compotes and set them throughout the house—in the cocktail area, out on the porch, atop circular tables that held the favors, and in any corner that needed an injection of color *(center)*.

To conceal the kitchen entry from the reception room, I propped up a three-paneled screen I'd rented from an antique boutique. Through the graceful floral patterns that filled its carved wooden frames, this freestanding triptych filtered light from one side of the room to the other. By partnering a marble countertop with a pair of cast-plaster columns, I crafted a much-needed bar station, then garnished it with an explosion of eucalyptus stems. The fluid lines of the trumpet vase, leading from a tight base to a wide mouth, caused the bulk of branches to span out into a small canopy *(bottom)*.

In a room illuminated solely by candles, plants will disappear as darkness falls. I recommend lighting large, deeply shaded arrangements. Actually, the impact of just about any arrangement is improved by planned lighting. For our eucalyptus fronds, we set a simple can light (available at any hardware store) on the floor beneath the bar. Its beam splashed shadows of the plant's elliptical leaves on the walls and up to the ceiling.

A simple stone hearth situated on the sunporch provided one of the reception's most romantic spots. Attended to by an "official" stoker from the catering staff, trained in the fine art of fire management, the fire

roared at a perfect pitch all night. The fireplace had no mantel, so to suit it up for the occasion, I fashioned a glittering garland from about forty mercury-glass ornaments *(page 222)*. Each one had a loop through which I threaded a forty-inch piece of wire, twisting it in half for extra strength. The combined widths of the silvery spheres reduced the workable length of the doubled wire to about ten inches. Once all ornaments were on board, I began to braid them together. Large globes marked either end of the swag, and smaller baubles filled the space between *(page 223, top)*. To lift and position the reflective wreath, have two helpers on hand, and use additional wire loops to hang each end from masonry nails anchored in the mantel.

I found these silver spirals and whirligigs so festive that I also nested a clutch into a silver compote bowl and displayed them as a scintillating centerpiece in the entrance hall.

Into the Woods on a Snowy Evening

Dashing through the snow in a one-horse open sleigh, the newly re-wed duo made their way to a quaint honeymoon cottage down the lane *(opposite)*. To keep the couple snug and cozy for the short ride, we warmed blankets indoors until the last minute. Lush camellia garlands draped the backboard of the coach, and faceted chandelier crystals *(top)* strung from thin silken ribbons chimed a charmed tune as the two drove off into the enchanted forest.

FAVORS

A wedding favor may not be mandatory, but it's one of the most memorable and gracious gestures at a reception. During the Middle Ages, guests vied for the bride's garters or ribbons, hoping to take home a bit of her good luck. In Victorian England, they often left a reception gifted with a new pair of kid gloves—the idea being that the newlyweds wanted all of their loved ones to feel warm and well-dressed. As thoughtful tokens of affection, favors tell friends and family that their presence is greatly appreciated. And I find that it's often the couple who benefits the most from these sentimental items. Years later, the precious talismans can be counted on to conjure up tender memories of the happy day. The options are endless, but whatever you choose to share with your guests, be sure to make it personal. Whether it's an

L'amour toujours! Give each guest a tiny tote. Papermaker Marie-Celeste Edwards recycles all sorts of ephemera in her pulp—billets-doux, birthday cards, cotton socks. Waxed twine ties the straw loops to the hand-folded satchels. Calligrapher Harriet Rose embellished the bags with impressionistic violet bouquets and a message in the language of love. Line the little purses with pretty tissue paper, then tuck candy kisses, scented candles, or a note of thanks inside.

original poem or a crisply folded origami swan (a wonderfully romantic image, because these elegant birds mate for life), the most gratifying favors send the message that the couple has taken the time to think about their guests.

Pretty favors dress up a table. If they're individually labeled, set one at each place. Or dedicate a table by the door to favors. Post a decorative sign encouraging guests to help themselves, or if quantity control is a concern, assign someone in your wedding party to distribute the gifts on your behalf.

Sign of the Dove: In lieu of a slice of groom's cake, baker Cheryl Kleinman frosted minty fondant petits fours. Calligrapher Stephannie Barba labeled glassine envelopes in green ink, and I sealed the sweet packets with satin ribbons—just like the peace offering delivered by the dove. For economy's sake, such pouches can serve a dual function: place card and favor *(opposite)*. Sugared almonds are always in season. In fact, some cultures consider these symbols of fertility indispensable to the wedding celebration. Almonds can be custom-colored to match any palette. Ask your cake baker, or look for a confectioner to accommodate your needs. Ricki Arno, renowned for her miniature detailing, iced white almonds with hearts, bows, and the couple's initials in golden and pearled hues *(top)*. Pastel treats in vintage silver sugar bowls are meant to be enjoyed at the reception *(bottom)*.

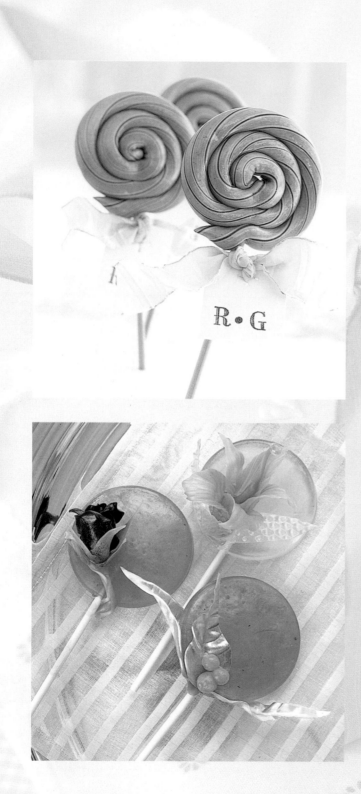

R · G

Is there anything more charming and childlike than a lollipop? Weddings make us feel young at heart, and few items embody this spirit better. I found the striped spirals at a neighborhood candy shop, and dressed them up with paper tags rubber-stamped with the couple's initials. To tie the tags to each wooden stick, I threaded yellow ribbon through an eighth-of-an-inch punched hole *(top)*. Chocolatier Steven Klc made translucent sugar suckers through a technique known as pulling *(bottom)*. Inquire about your baker's range—many are trained to make candy. Snow globes present a world of opportunities: photos, pressed flowers, or original illustrations can be slipped inside a plastic sleeve that splits the viewing field. Stephannie Barba customized these domes with holiday images, the couple's names, and the date *(opposite)*. I like to use them as both favors and place cards.

The sweet grains we call sugar can be rolled, molded, melted, pressed, piped, and painted in a multitude of ways. Gail Watson, a master of the medium, has perfected the sugar box *(opposite)*. Its base is made of granulated sugar and its lid cut from fondant and encrusted with more glittering grains. A four-inch-square container holds a quartet of chocolate truffles. Confection queen Betty van Norstrand coaxes a breathtakingly realistic blush from her cane creations. In this delicate posy of sweet peas, an embossed fondant doily wraps tender, tinted blooms *(top)*. Sugar boxes can also be crafted from solid fondant *(bottom)*. Royal icing trims a shallow, heart-shaped box and adheres the stems of hand-colored pastillage pansies to the lid. Valentine mints fill the interior. Although sugar boxes can sit on knick-knack shelves for months, think about using them to serve an extravagant dessert of mousse.

Despite all the modern methods of communicating, nothing can take the place of a thank-you note. It's so easy to jot down a few words on a blank page, and if you start weeks before your wedding day, the task won't seem so daunting. My own penmanship is atrocious, so I prefer to employ a calligrapher for the job. With pretty script, the card itself becomes a keepsake. Maria Thomas of Pendragon penned thank-yous in a swirling Spencerian script, then embellished them with painted flowers that complement the pink Japanese rice-paper cakes *(opposite)*. Stephannie Barba's casual calligraphy made a good match with the plain kraft-paper packaging of a porcelain ornament *(top)*. She also wrote the notes for an ornate wire tote that held home-baked gingerbread cookies swathed in remnants of gold silk *(bottom)*. When favors are this precious, order a few extras for absentees—and one for yourself!

credits

A page-by-page listing of each product and provider featured in this book follows. Once you determine the identity of the item photographed, use the resource list (where services and products are listed alphabetically by category) to obtain the contact numbers for every listing. Vintage and antique products are one-of-a-kind items, seek similar items at flea markets and antique dealers.

HALF-TITLE PAGE: a pair of marzipan pears, Kim Jurado, Brooklyn, NY; pleated paper pastry cups, New York Cake & Baking Distributors, NY, NY; glass compote, Eastern Accent International at Matsu, Boston, MA; calligraphy, Ellen W. Weldon Designs, NY, NY; dinner plate, Service Party Rentals, NY, NY. **TITLE PAGE:** a formal place setting of vintage sterling silver flatware, charger, salad, place card holder, Tudor Rose Antiques, NY, NY; vintage mono-grammed linen napkin, Trouvaille Francaise, NY, NY; calligraphy, Anna Pinto, Hoboken, NJ. **COPYRIGHT PAGE:** spring blooms left to right, dogwood, narcissus, muscari, cherry blossoms, pansy,

lilac, arranged by Christopher Bassett, NY, NY; green glazed vase, Aletha Soulé available through the Loom Company, NY, NY; striped glass vase, Penelope Wurr at the Loom Company, NY, NY; geometric etched goblet, Eastern Accent International available at Matsu, Boston, MA.

INTRODUCTION

PAGE 8: champagne flutes, Abigails, Alexandria, LA.; assorted crystalized sugars, Dean & Deluca, NY, NY. **PAGE 10:** *top:* tin box, USCAN at Paper Access, NY, NY; embossed silver foil seal, Gift Box Corporation of America, NY, NY; mesh ribbon, Brimar, Highland Park, IL; calligraphy, Ellen W. Weldon Designs, NY, NY; shadow stripe organza napkin, Todd Moore Home, NY, NY; sterling silver napkin ring, Trudy Borenstein-Segiura at Deborah Shapiro, NY, NY; sterling flatware, Gorham, Lenox Brands, Lawrenceville, NJ; silver charger, Service Party Rental, NY, NY. *middle:* dogwood blossom box, Two Design Group, Dallas, TX; satin ribbon, Offray &

Son, Chester, NJ. *bottom:* peach infused champagne cocktails; etched tumblers, Sahara Morrocan Imports, NY, NY; peach marzipan garnish, Kim Jurado, Brooklyn, NY; serving tray, Pottery Barn, NY, NY. **PAGE 11:** *top:* tin lanterns, tea lights, Ikea, Elizabeth, NJ. *middle:* place cards laced with a sprig of lily-of-the-valley, calligraphy and illustration, Stephannie Barba, NY, NY; tablecloth, Just Linens, NY, NY. *bottom:* crystal-bead wedding cake as centerpiece, Yona Levine, NY, NY; vintage depression glass plate. **PAGE 12:** *top:* lamp sconces rest upside down as candle hurricanes, Olde Good Things, NY, NY. *middle:* vintage linen embroidered coasters. *bottom:* mono-gramed sterling card holder, Tudor Rose Antiques, NY, NY; calligraphy, Anna Pinto, Hoboken, NJ; champagne flute, Baccarat, NY, NY; table-cloth, Angel Threads, Brooklyn, NY. **PAGE 13:** assorted white linen table-cloths, *top to bottom:* guipure lace by Ruth Fischl, NY, NY; embroidered organza, Ruth Fischl, NY, NY; embroidered cotton detailed with three-dimensional organza

roses, Todd Moore Home, NY, NY; windowpane organza, Ruth Fischl; burn-out velvet with fringe, Ruth Fischl; ball-room chair, Service Party Rental, NY, NY. **PAGE 14:** *top:* pomander centerpiece of white roses nests on hydrangea petals, Todd Fiscus, Two Design Group, Dallas, TX; silver candy dish, Hôtel, Darien, CT. *middle:* chair back slipcover, Angel Threads, Brooklyn, NY; ballroom chair, Service Party Rental, NY, NY. *bottom:* strapless bridal gown, Edgardo Bonilla through Creative Design Management, Haddonfield, NJ; parasol, Lippincott, Ringoes, NJ. **PAGE 15:** *top:* floating candles, Nelson Candles available at The Candle Shop, NY, NY; stone bird bath, Treillage, NY, NY. *middle:* cham-pagne flutes, Service Party Rental, NY, NY. *bottom:* iced cookies, Newton Pryce, Great Performances, NY, NY; sterling compote, Tudor Rose Antiques, NY, NY. **PAGE 16:** escort cards, Crane & Company, Dalton, MA; calligraphy, Stephannie Barba, NY, NY. **PAGE 17:** *top:* votives wrapped with hand-printed hand made paper, Arak-Kanofsky Studios,

Easton, PA; table linens, Angel Threads, Brooklyn, NY. *middle*: anemone bouquet, Priscilla Schaefer, Glorimundi, NY, NY. *bottom*: monogrammed hotel silver flatware, Pottery Barn, NY, NY.

SPRING

PAGE 23: *top to bottom*: bride, Linette Dunbar; groom, Grant Aumell; hair and makeup, Kim DePaolera, Totowa, NJ; bouquet, Two Design Group, Dallas, TX; bridal gown, Amsale, NY, NY; cystal crown, Rados Protic, NY, NY; satin ribbon choker, Midori, Seattle, WA; morning suit, Lord West, Woodside, NY; tie, Gene Meyer, NY, NY; champagne flute, Baccarat, NY, NY. **PAGE 24:** *top , left to right*: Todd Fiscus, Raegan B. McKinney of Two Design Group, Dallas, TX. *middle*: Cheryl Kleinman, Brooklyn, NY; *bottom left to right*: Cesar Sanchez, Leonardo Iturregui, Edward Magel, executive chef, and Susan Holland of Susan Holland Events and Catering Company, NY, NY. **PAGE 28-29:** floral garland, Two Design Group, Dallas, TX. **PAGE 30:** *left*: citrus and herb-scented olives, Susan Holland, NY, NY; gold plated saucer, Ostafin Designs NY, NY. *center*: seeded breadsticks and romesco sauce, Susan Holland; gold porcelain

serving tray, Ostafin Designs. *right*: floral dessert dish, William Wayne, NY, NY. **PAGE 31:** tablecloth and napkins, Ruth Fischl, NY, NY; gold flatware, individual salt and pepper shakers, cut crystal wine goblets, Service Party Rental NY, NY; dove knife rests, Two Design Group, Dallas, TX; raspberry charger, Angèle Parlange for Abigails, Alexandria, LA; chintz salad plate, Bernardaud, NY, NY; etched stemware, Abigails; place cards, calligraphy, Caroline Paget Leake, Brooklyn, NY; centerpiece, Two Design Group; shaved artichoke hearts and parmesan, chevre crotin and breadstick, Susan Holland, NY, NY. **PAGE 32:** table number calligraphy, Caroline Paget Leake, Brooklyn, NY. **PAGE 33:** *left*: place card calligraphy, Caroline Paget Leake, Brooklyn, NY. *right*: flatware, Service Party Rental, NY, NY. **PAGE 34:** custom table linens and mini-skirt slip covers, Ruth Fischl, NY, NY; fabric, B & J Fabrics, NY, NY; rental tables, Service Party Rental, NY, NY. **PAGE 36:** beverage garnishes in assorted pressed glass bowls, William Wayne, NY, NY; rose centerpiece, Two Design Group, Dallas, TX; Venetian glass compote, Dorian Webb, NY, NY; plaid pink jacquard tablecloth, Just Linens, NY, NY. **PAGE 37:** champagne

flutes, Baccarat, NY, NY; heart-shaped silver sipper spoons, Gorham, Lenox Brands, Lawrenceville, NJ; cherry shrug with rose bud garnish, Susan Holland, NY, NY; tablecloth, Ruth Fischl, NY, NY; vintage monogrammed linen cocktail napkins. **PAGE 38-39:** pitchers and contents *left to right*: pink lemonade in hobnail glass pitcher available at William Wayne, NY, NY; elder flower tisane; ginger iced tea, cherry shrug, chamomile mint iced tea in one of a kind vintage glass pitchers and carafe available at Ostafin Designs, NY, NY, beverages, Susan Holland, NY, NY; gold wire, Brimar, Highland Park, IL; satin ribbons, Midori, Seattle, WA; tablecloth, Just Linens, NY, NY. **PAGE 40:** Jumbo lump crab meat on noodle crisp, Susan Holland, NY, NY. **PAGE 42:** *top*: smoked salmon on sticky rice garnished with rose petal, Susan Holland, NY, NY. *middle*: Vietnamese chicken in rice paper, Susan Holland. *bottom*: mango with yogurt in sesame barquette, Susan Holland; gold porcelain tray, Ostafin Designs, NY, NY. **PAGE 43:** warm asparagus salad, Susan Holland, NY, NY; vintage porcelain plate, Ostafin Designs, NY, NY. **PAGE 44:** *left*: salmon *bouillabaisse*, Susan Holland, NY, NY; vintage gold porcelain, Ostafin Designs, NY, NY. *right*: lamb *pot au*

feu, Susan Holland; porcelain, Ostafin Designs; flatware, Service Party Rental, NY, NY; linens, Ruth Fischl, NY, NY. **PAGE 45:** a trio of sweet bites, Susan Holland, NY, NY; vintage porcelain saucer, Ostafin Designs, NY, NY. **PAGE 46:** *left*: hand-sculpted sugar vase as cake topper, Cheryl Kleinman Cakes, Brooklyn, NY. *right*: cake slice, Cheryl Kleinman; panna cotta, Susan Holland, NY, NY; porcelain cake plates, Ostafin Designs, NY, NY; taffeta candy-strip tablecloth, Ruth Fischl, NY, NY. **PAGE 47:** wedding cake, Cheryl Kleinman Cakes, Brooklyn, NY; embroidered organza cloth, Just Linens, NY, NY. **PAGE 48:** handmade paper tote, Marie-Celeste Edwards of D.H. Productions Paper Mill & Press, Kent Lakes, NY; organza ribbon, Midori, Seattle, WA; tablecloth, Ruth Fischl, NY, NY. **PAGE 49:** invitation with monogram, r.s.v.p. card and addressed envelope, calligraphy and design by Caroline Paget Leake, Brooklyn, NY. **PAGE 50:** *left*: formalwear, Lord West, Woodside, NY; tie, Gene Meyer, NY, NY; boutonniere, Two Design Group, Dallas, TX. *center and right*: bridesmaids' bouquets, Two Design Group; French-braided satin ribbon, Midori, Seattle, WA; crystal ornaments, M & J Trimming, NY, NY.

PAGE 51: bridal bouquet of roses, sweet pea, lily of the valley, Two Design Group, Dallas, TX; Swarovski crystals, Cinderella Flowers, NY, NY; gold wire, Metalliferous, NY, NY. PAGE 52: hydrangea orb, Two Design Group, Dallas, TX; anitque stone garden pedestal, Treillage, NY, NY; satin ribbons, Midori, Seattle, WA. PAGE 53: vintage iron garden chairs; silk mini-skirt slip cover, Ruth Fischl, NY, NY; chair back floral flourish, Two Design Group, Dallas, TX. PAGE 54: details of floral arrangement, Two Design Group, Dallas, TX. PAGE 55: floral arrangement, Two Design Group, Dallas, TX; preserved butterflies, Schoepfer Natural Artifacts, NY, NY. PAGE 56: 1939 Buick Road Master Rolls Royce, Black Tie Limousine, Farmingville, NY; photography location, Old Westbury Gardens, Old Westbury, NY.

TABLE DETAILS

PAGE 58: pewter candlesticks, Dansk International Designs for Lenox Brands, Lawrenceville, NJ; pastel candles, Creative Candles available at The Candle Shop, NY, NY; wired sugar flowers, Jan Kish, La Petite Fleur, Worthington, Ohio. PAGE 60: *top*: sterling salt cellars, Tudor Rose Antiques, NY, NY. *bottom*: monogrammed sterling napkin bands, tray, Tudor

Rose Antiques; linen napkins, Trouvaille Francaise, NY, NY. PAGE 61: sterling flatware, Buccellati, NY, NY; vintage Limoge porcelain, salt & pepper shakers, etched stemware, Ostafin Design, NY, NY; place card and menu, Ellen W. Welden Designs, NY, NY; napkin and tablecloth, Just Linens, NY, NY. PAGE 62: flatware, Hotel, Darien, CT; vintage transferware plate, John Derian, NY, NY; pique napkin, placemat, Angel Threads, Brooklyn, NY; place card, paper napkin band, calligraphy and illustration, Stephannie Barba, NY, NY; glass tumbler, Crate & Barrel, Chicago, IL. PAGE 63: *top*: calligraphy, Anna Pinto, Hoboken, NJ. *bottom*, knife, Gorham, Lenox Brands, Lawrenceville, NJ; knife rest, Lunares, San Francisco, CA. PAGE 64: calligraphy, Anna Pinto, Hoboken, NJ; ribbon, Hanah Silk, Los Angeles, CA; napkin and tablecloth, Just Linens, NY, NY; flatware, Kirk Stieff, Lenox Brands, Lawrenceville, NJ; plate, Service Party Rentals, NY, NY; heart tuille, Newton Pryce, Great Performances, NY, NY. PAGE 65: pewter compote, Dansk International Designs for Lenox Brands, Lawrenceville, NJ; napkin, cloth, Just Linens, NY, NY; "Tuscany" dinner plate, Service Party Rental, NY, NY; flatware, Hotel,

Darien, CT; glassware, Crate & Barrel, Chicago, IL; calligraphy and illustration, Stephannie Barba, NY, NY; squares of white kraft butcher's paper as overlay. PAGE 66: tin letter, C.I.T.E., NY, NY; linen napkin, Just Linens, NY, NY; ribbon, Offray & Son, Chester, NJ. PAGE 67: silk napkins, MU/H; monogrammed ribbons, Monograms by Emily, NY, NY; satin ribbon, Midori, Seattle, WA; silk ribbon, Midori, Seattle, WA; Venetian glass ornament, Dorian Webb, NY, NY. PAGE 68: *top*: blank place cards, Julie Holcomb Printers, Emeryville, CA. *bottom*: quill, ink, French Corner, Elmsford, NY, gold edged place cards, Crane & Company, Dalton, MA. PAGE 69: place cards, Maria Thomas, Pendragon, Ink, Whitinsville, MA. PAGE 70: calligraphy, Stephannie Barba, NY, NY; blank card, Crane & Company; napkin, MU/H, NY, NY; gold chocolate rings, Crispo, imported from Italy by Lauria Food Enterprises, Howard Beach, NY. PAGE 71: *top*: calligraphy, Bernard Maisner, Bayhead, NJ. *bottom*: handmade place cards with custom water mark, Marie-Celeste Edwards of DH Productions Paper Mill & Press, Kent Lakes, NY; calligraphy, Stephannie Barba, NY, NY. PAGE 72: hand-embossed folders for menus or invitations, Zelda Tannenbaum of Hollis

Hills Mill, Hollis Hills, NY; calligraphy, Stephannie Barba, NY, NY. PAGE 73: calligraphy and menu design, Jennifer Viviano of Viviano Designs, Portland, OR. PAGE 74: table numbers, Hotel, Darien, CT. PAGE 75: *top*: small black boards, Cite, NY, NY; lettering, Stephannie Barba, NY, NY; silver cups, Kirk Stieff, Lenox Brands, Lawrenceville, NJ. *bottom*: sugar table number, Steven Klc, McLean, VA. PAGE 76: *top*: letter press coasters, Purgatory Pie Press, NY, NY; *bottom*: calligraphy, illustration, Stephannie Barba, NY, NY. PAGE 77: doilies, Broadway Panhandler, NY, NY; calligraphy, Stephannie Barba, NY, NY.

SUMMER

PAGE 83: *top to bottom*: bride, Martina Gates; bridesmaids, Tracy Trevett and Regina Whitaker; hair and makeup artist, Rick Teale, NY, NY; bridal bouquet, Preston Bailey Events, NY, NY; bridal gown, Wearkstatt, NY, NY; bridesmaids' sarongs, Malatesta available at Calypso, NY, NY; spaghetti strap tank tops, Anne Fontaine, NY, NY. PAGE 84: *top to bottom*: Peter Callahan, Callahan Catering, NY, NY; Preston Bailey, NY, NY; Margaret Braun, NY, NY. PAGE 85: *top to bottom*: Todd Moore, NY, NY; detail summer reception; Geoff Howell, NY, NY. **PAGE 88:** cafe tables, chairs, Geoff Howell Studio, NY, NY; bistro cloths, Todd Moore Home, NY, NY; floral trees, Preston Bailey, NY, NY. **PAGE 89:** teak lounge chairs, table, Chista, NY, NY; custom parasols, Geoff Howell Studio, NY, NY; pillows, Sylvia Heisel, NY, NY; orchids, Preston Bailey, NY, NY; champagne flute, Dickey Glass, Williamstown, WV. **PAGE 90:** menu design, Kayo Der Sarkissian, NY, NY; napkin, Todd Moore Home, NY, NY; lustreware dinner plate, Swid Powell, NY, NY; lacquerware charger, Carnevale, Memphis, TN. **PAGE 91:** centerpiece, votives, Preston Bailey, NY, NY; custom velum chandelier, Geoff Howell Studio, NY, NY; table, chairs, Service Party Rental, NY, NY; custom tablecloth, napkins Todd Moore Home, NY, NY; stemware, Dickey Glass, Williamstown, WV; sterling flatware, Gense, NY, NY; lustreware dinner plate, Swid Powell, NY, NY; lacquerware charger, Carnevale, Memphis, TN; green leaf saucers, William Wayne, NY, NY. **PAGE 92-93:** custom tent, parasols, lanterns, Geoff Howell Studio, NY, NY; table, chairs, Service Party Rentals, NY, NY; tablecloths, chair cushions, napkins, Todd Moore Home, NY, NY; flowers, Preston

Bailey, NY, NY; incense spiral, Eclectic Imports, Los Angeles, CA. **PAGE 94:** assorted stemware, tumblers, Dickey Glass, Williamstown, WV. **PAGE 95:** *left:* pitchers, Dickey Glass, Williamstown, WV; condiment saucer, Aletha Soule at The Loom Company, NY, NY. *right:* custom bamboo bar: bamboo, Preston Bailey, NY, NY; frosted plexiglass top, Geoff Howell Studio, NY, NY; lime pyramid, Preston Bailey; pitchers, stemware, Dickey Glass. **PAGE 96:** *top:* mini grills, hors d'oeuvres, Peter Callahan Catering, NY, NY; oblong saucer, Marek Cecula available at Mxyplyzyk, NY, NY; *middle:* ice block frozen with flowers, Ice Sculpture Designs, Deer Park, NY; raw bar, Peter Callahan Catering. *bottom:* hors d'ouevres, Peter Callahan Catering; bamboo spoons, green glazed bowls, William Wayne, NY, NY. **PAGE 97:** custom bamboo bar: bamboo, Preston Bailey, NY, NY; frosted plexiglass top, Geoff Howell Studio, NY, NY; lanterns, Geoff Howell Studio; raw bar hors d'ouevres, Peter Callahan Catering, NY, NY; large leaf plate, Christian Tortu available at Takashimaya, NY, NY; long saucers, Marek Cecula available at Mxyplyzyk, NY, NY; assorted condiment bowls, utensils, William Wayne, NY, NY. **PAGE 98:**

stemware, Dickey Glass, Williamstown, WV; cocktails, Peter Callahan Catering, NY, NY; napkin, Todd Moore Home, NY, NY; sterling tray, Towle Silversmiths, East Boston, MA. **PAGE 99:** *left:* centerpieces, Preston Bailey, NY, NY; laquerware plate under centerpieces, Carnavale, Memphis, TN; tablecloths, chair back swags, Todd Moore Home, NY, NY; tables, chairs, Geoff Howell Studio, NY, NY; glassware, votives, Dickey Glass, Williamstown, WV; cocktails, hors d'ouevres, Peter Callahan Catering, NY, NY. *right:* hors d'ouevres, Peter Callahan Catering; leaf plate, William Wayne, NY, NY; tablecloth, Todd Moore Home. **PAGE 100:** lobster-potato petits fours on cucumber lattice, Peter Callahan Catering, NY, NY. **PAGE 102:** *left:* plaintain chicken with papaya, Peter Callahan Catering, NY, NY; handmade porcelain plate, Soendergaard available through Camden Lane, NY, NY. *right:* corn blinis, Peter Callahan Catering, NY, NY, tray, Jill Rosenwald, Boston, MA. **PAGE 103:** orchid pyramid, votives Preston Bailey, NY, NY; heirloom tomato soup, Peter Callahan Catering, NY, NY; soup bowl, Crate & Barrel; stemware, Dickey Glass, Williamstown, WV; leaf dish, William Wayne, NY, NY; sterling flatware,

Gense, NY, NY; vintage glass leaf as knife rest; napkin, tablecloth, Todd Moore Home, NY, NY; lustreware dinner plate, Swid Powell, NY, NY; lacquerware charger, Carnevale, Memphis, TN. **PAGE 104:** grilled fillet, vegetables, Peter Callahan Catering, NY, NY; plate, Daniel Levy Ceramics, NY, NY. **PAGE 105:** grilled fruit, sorbets, Peter Callahan Catering, NY, NY; lustreware plate, Swid Powell, NY, NY. **PAGE 106-107:** wedding cake, Margaret Braun, NY, NY, tablecloth, Todd Moore Home, NY, NY; table, Service Party Rental, NY, NY; custom parasol, Geoff Howell Studio, NY, NY. **PAGE 108:** ballroom chairs, Service Party Rental, NY, NY; cushions, Todd Moore Home, NY, NY. **PAGE 109:** invitation design, Kayo Der Sarkissian, NY, NY; velum, Kate's Paperie, NY, NY. **PAGE 110:** *left:* tent pennant, Geoff Howell Studio, NY, NY; *right:* incense spiral, Eclectic Imports, Los Angeles, CA. **PAGE 111:** custom chandelier, Geoff Howell Studio, NY, NY. **PAGE 112:** bouquet, Preston Bailey, NY, NY. **PAGE 113:** *top:* bamboo table, Chista, NY, NY; bouquet, Preston Bailey, NY, NY; ribbon, Midori, Seattle, WA. *bottom:* bouquet, Preston Bailey. **PAGE 114:** centerpieces, Preston Bailey, NY, NY;

lacquerware charger, Carnevale, Memphis, TN; tablecloth, Todd Moore Home, NY, NY. **PAGE 115:** straw paddle fans, basket, Pearl River Mart, NY, NY; graphic design, Kayo Der Sarkissian, NY, NY; satin ribbon, Offray & Son, Chester, NJ. **PAGE 117:** teak bed, table, bowl, Chista, NY, NY; bed linens, ABC Carpet & Home, NY, NY; cotton gauze, B&J Fabrics, NY, NY; orchids, Preston Bailey, NY, NY.

FLOWERS

PAGE 118: bell jar, Abigails, Alexandria, LA; etched glass tumbler, Eastern Accent International at Matsu, Boston, MA; sterling flatware, Wallace Silversmiths, East Boston, MA; silver tray, Towle Silversmiths, East Boston, MA; satin ribbon, Offray & Son, Chester, NJ; flowers, Christopher Bassett, NY, NY. **PAGE 120:** *top:* spring centerpiece, Todd Fiscus, Two Design Group, Dallas, TX; gilt urn, Ostafin Design, NY, NY. *bottom:* summery centerpiece, Christopher Bassett, NY, NY; silver tray, Hotel, Darien CT. **PAGE 121:** centerpiece, Reagan McKinney, Two Design Group, Dallas, TX; Venetian glass compote, Dorian Webb, NY, NY. **PAGE 122:** fall centerpiece, Christopher Bassett, NY, NY. **PAGE 123:** minia-

ture pine, Priscilla Schaeffer, Glorimundi, NY, NY; galvanized buckets, Ikea, Elizabeth, NJ; mesh ribbon, Vaban International, Atlanta, GA. **PAGE 124:** vase, Soendergaard Design available through Camden Lane, NY, NY; table runner, Daisy Hill, Louisville, KY; floral design, Christopher Bassett, NY, NY. **PAGE 124:** *top:* floral design, Christopher Bassett, NY, NY; basket, Simon Pearce, Quechee, VT; ballroom chair, Service Party Rental, NY, NY. *bottom:* floral design, Christoher Bassett, NY, NY; preserved butterfly, Schoepfer Natural Artifacts, NY, NY; table cloth, Just Linens, NY, NY. **PAGE 125:** *top:* nosegay, Christopher Bassett, NY, NY; ribbon, Offray & Son, Chester, NJ; plate, Alethea Soule available through The Loom Company, NY, NY; sterling flatware, Gorham, Lenox Brands, Lawrenceville, NJ; place card and calligraphy, Anna Pinto, Hoboken, NJ; napkin, Todd Moore Home, NY, NY. *bottom:* floral design, Christopher Bassett. **PAGE 126:** floral design, Christopher Bassett, NY, NY; ribbon, Brimar, Highland Park, IL; mesh wrapped votive, One Thousand Cranes, NY, NY; escort cards, Caroline Paget Leake, Brooklyn, NY; tablecloth, MU/H, NY, NY. **PAGE 128:** *top:*

dogwood box, Raegan McKinney, Two Design Group, Dallas, TX; tin box, US Can, Baltimore, MD; ribbon, Offray & Son, Chester, NJ; *bottom:* sugared flowers, Jan Kish, La Petite Fleur, Worthington, Ohio. **PAGE 129:** floral design, Christopher Bassett, NY, NY; preserved butterfly, Schoepfer Natural Artifacts, NY, NY; glass cake plate, Ostafin Designs, NY, NY.

FALL

PAGE 135: *top to bottom:* bride, Magdalena Mickiewicz; groom, Steve Benisty; hair and makeup artist, Patricia Bowden-Luccardi, Stamford, CT; bridal gown, Wearkstatt, NY, NY; cashmere sweater, N.Peal, NY, NY; throw, Churchill Weavers, Berea, KY; earrings, Meryl Waitz, NY, NY; shoes, Vanessa Noel, NY, NY; his suit, Calvin Klein, NY, NY; shoes, Cole Haan, Yarmouth, ME; bridal bouquet and boutonniere, Florals of Waterford, Saddle River, NJ. **PAGE 136:** *top to bottom:* Katie and Michael Meeks, Florals of Waterford, Saddle River, NJ; Rosemary Littman, Rosemary's Cakes, Teaneck, NJ; Daniel Mattrocce, DM Cuisine, NY, NY. **PAGE 140:** hand-painted sign, Mark Musters, NY, NY. **PAGE 141:** frame, Gill & Lagodich Gallery, NY, NY;

bittersweet bouquet, Florals of Waterford, Saddle River, NJ; chenile oriental runner, Emdee International; iron chair, B & B International, NY, NY. **PAGE 142-143:** grapevine garland, Florals of Waterford, Saddle River, NJ; lanterns, Sahara Moroccan Imports, NY, NY; iron chair, pedestal, chandeliers, Treillage, NY, NY; chenile oriental runners, Emdee International, Atlanta, GA; iron table, Tin Man, Cold Spring, NY. **PAGE 144:** *left:* antique wood and brass flatware, Pottery Barn; silk napkins, Ann Gish, Newbury Park, CA. *center:* embossed, handmade paper coasters, Zelda Tannenbaum, Hollis Hills Mill, Hollis Hills, NY; calligraphy, Lori Saucier, The Elegant Pen, Suffern, NY; etched tumbler, Sahara Moroccan Imports, NY, NY. *right:* glazed numbered tile, Moravian Pottery and Tile Works, Doylestown, PA. **PAGE 145:** round tables, Service Party Rental, NY, NY; stenciled monogram on short silk table skirt, Pintura Studio, NY, NY; long silk skirts and ultra suede overlays, Ann Gish, Newbury Park, CA; chandeliers, Treillage, NY, NY; floral centerpieces, Florals of Waterford, Saddle River, NJ; lantern, Sahara Moroccan Imports, NY, NY; chenile oriental runners, Emdee International, Atlanta, GA. **PAGE 146:** buttermilk biscuit, DM Cuisine, NY, NY; copper plate, Manhattan Fruittier, NY, NY; butter knife, Tudor Rose Antiques, NY, NY. **PAGE 147:** centerpiece, Florals of Waterford, Saddle River, NJ; vintage pottery, Crooksville American Art Pottery available through Florals of Waterford; table, Service Party Rental, NY, NY; suede overlays, silk skirts, napkins, Ann Gish, Newbury Park, CA; flatware, Pottery Barn, NY, NY; apple, pear candles, Beeskep II, Johnstown, NY; tumblers, Sahara Moroccan Imports, NY, NY; pillows, Kashmir, NY, NY. **PAGE 148:** *left:* stemware, Lalique, NY, NY; apple cider, DM Cuisine, NY, NY; embossed coasters, Zelda Tannenbaum, Hollis Hills Mill, Hollis Hills, NY; gilt-framed mirror, Gill & Lagodich Gallery, NY, NY. *right::* cut-glass pitcher, William Wayne, NY, NY; smooth pitcher, Simon Pearce, Quechee, VT; vintage glass milk bottles, Once Upon A Table, Pittsfield, MA. **PAGE 149:** prosecco di Valdobbiandene and prosecco Sergio Mionetto bottled by Mionetto Spumanti SRL and imported by Prima Qualita, available at Windsor Wine Shop, NY, NY. **PAGE 150:** wild rice pancake hors d'eouvres, DM Cuisine, NY, NY; skeletonized magnolia leaves, Loose Ends, Kreizer,

OR; gold lacquer bowl, Asiaphile, Glendale, CA; wood tray, Calvin Klein Home, NY, NY. **PAGE 152:** *top:* acorn squash soup, DM Cuisine, NY, NY; sake cups, Anthropologie, NY, NY; wood spoon, Manhattan Fruittier, NY, NY; metal tray, Calvin Klein Home, NY, NY. *center:* roasted chestnuts, DM Cuisine, NY, NY; vellum bags made from sheets of paper available at Paper Access, NY, NY. *bottom:* grilled pizzas, DM Cuisine, NY, NY; napkin, Just Linens, NY, NY. **PAGE 153:** grilled pizzas, DM Cuisine, NY, NY; barbeque grill, Service Party Rental, NY, NY. **PAGE 154:** centerpiece, Florals of Waterford, Saddle River, NJ; glazed urn, Burts Cason, Baton Rouge, LA; vintage round wood frame as base frame for centerpiece, Gill & Lagodich Gallery, NY, NY; buffet, DM Cuisine, NY, NY; braised red cabbage served in gold leaf under glass vessel, Anthropologie, NY, NY; roasted vegetables served in copper bowl, Manhattan Fruittier, NY, NY; frisee salad served in pie crust bowl, Pot Luck Studios, Accord, NY; grilled pheasant served in wood tray, Calvin Klein Home, NY, NY; copper sheeting, Metalliferous, NY, NY; cranberry-pear compote served in glazed bowl, Pot Luck Studios; pot pie served in copper pot,

Bridge Kitchen Supplies, NY, NY; hand-forged iron utensils, Antiqua available through Isadora & Mizrahi, NY, NY; silk tablecloth, Ann Gish, Newbury Park, CA. **PAGE 155:** *top:* oven-roasted late-harvest vegetables, DM Cuisine, NY, NY; hammered copper bowl, small copper plate, Manhattan Fruittier, NY, NY; utensils, Antiqua available through Isadora & Mizrahi, NY, NY. *bottom:* serving, DM Cuisine; bronze plate, Calvin Klein Home, NY, NY; utensils, Pottery Barn; silk napkin, Ann Gish, Newbury Park, CA. **PAGE 156:** carmelized pears, DM Cuisine, NY, NY; plate, Takashimaya, NY, NY; tablecloth, napkin, Ann Gish, Newbury Park, CA. **PAGE 157:** ice-cream sandwiches, DM Cuisine, NY, NY; lacquer-ware tray, Asiaphile, Glendale, CA. **PAGE 158:** slice of buttercream cake, marzipan, Rosemary's Cakes, Teaneck, NJ; Chinese wood plates, Manhattan Fruittier, NY, NY. **PAGE 159:** buttercream wedding cake, Rosemary Littman, Rosemary's Cakes, Teaneck, NJ. **PAGE 160:** natural straw mesh bags, Joneses International, Walnut Creek, CA; apple and pear candles, Beeskep II, Johnstown, NY. **PAGE 161:** *left:* candles, Beeskep II, Johnstown, NY. right: invitation, Purgatory Pie Press, NY, NY. **PAGE 163:**

bouquet, Florals of Waterford, Saddle River, NJ; bridal gown, Wearkstatt, NY, NY; cashmere sweater, N.Peal, NY, NY. **PAGE 164:** *top:* centerpiece, Florals of Waterford, Saddle River, NJ; large glazed urn, Burts Cason, Baton Rouge, LA; utensils, Pottery Barn. *bottom:* bouquet, Florals of Waterford, Saddle River, NJ; ribbons, Mokuba; NY, NY; cloth, Ann Gish, Newbury Park, CA. **PAGE 165:** vintage 1957 Ford "Woody," thanks to owners Lynn and Jim Gregerson; "Just Married" clay letter tiles, Moravian Pottery & Tile Works, Doylestown, PA.

CONFECTIONS

PAGE 166: wedding cake cookies, Gail Watson Cake, NY, NY; silver tray, Towle Silversmiths, East Boston, MA. **PAGE 168:** iced button cookies, Patti Page, Baked Ideas, NY, NY; embroidered linen hankerchief, Lilien's Hankicards, Clinton, WA. **PAGE 169:** iced heart cookies, Ricki Arno, Rosie's Creations, NY, NY **PAGE 170:** gilded dessert plate, serving tray and filigree vase, Ostafin Designs, NY, NY; flowers, Two Design Group, Dallas, TX; Japanese confections, Minamoto Kiochoen, NY, NY. **PAGE 171:** *top:* iced sugar cubes, Ricki Arno, Rosie's Creations, NY, NY; sterling tongs, Tudor Rose Antiques, NY, NY. *bottom:*

sugar bowl, rose-decorated sugar cubes, Jan Kish, La Petite Fleur, Worthington, Ohio; vintage Limoge plate, Ostafin Designs, NY, NY; demitasse spoon, Tea For Two, Laguna Beach, CA. **PAGE 172:** *top & bottom:* petits fours, Cheryl Kleinman Cakes, Brooklyn, NY. **PAGE 173:** petits fours, Cheryl Kleinman Cakes, Brooklyn, NY; tray, Hôtel, Darien, CT. **PAGE 174:** cake, Polly Schoonmaker, Polly's Cakes, Portland, OR; sterling fork, Wallace Silversmiths, East Boston, MA; dessert plate, Service Party Rentals, NY, NY. **PAGE 175:** cake, Gail Watson Cakes, NY, NY. **PAGE 176:** jewel box cake, Jan Kish, La Petite Fleur, Worthington, OH; porcelain serving plate, Wedgwood, Wall, NJ. **PAGE 177:** *top:* cake, Ellen Baumwoll, Bijoux Doux, NY, NY; cake plate, Mariposa, Manchester, MA. *bottom:* cake, Polly Schoonmaker, Polly's Cakes, Portland, OR; cake plate, Rosenthal, Carlstadt, NJ; gingham cloth overlay, Todd Moore Home, NY, NY. **PAGE 178:** *top:* cake, Gail Watson Cakes, NY, NY; *bottom:* Ellen Baumwoll, Bijoux Doux, NY, NY. **PAGE 179:** mini wedding cakes, Gail Watson Cakes, NY, NY; doilies, Artifacts, Palestine, TX. **PAGE 180:** cake, Polly Schoonmaker, Polly's Cakes, Portland, OR;

handmade paper round, La Papeterie St-Armand, Montreal, Canada available at NY Central Art Supply, NY, NY; illustrator, Chistopher Bassett, NY, NY. **PAGE 181:** *top:* sandblasted glass rounds, Acme Sandblasting, NY, NY; design, Stephannie Barba, NY, NY. *bottom:* handmade paper round, La Papeterie St-Armand, Montreal, Canada available at NY Central Art Supply, NY, NY; calligraphy, Stephannie Barba. **PAGE 182:** cake, Margaret Braun, NY, NY; cake plate, Abigails, Alexandria, LA.

WINTER

PAGE 189: *top to bottom:* bride, Michelle Childs; groom, Star Childs; flower girl, Quincy Childs; hair and makeup stylist, Patricia Bowden-Luccardi, Stamford, CT; bridal gown, Reem Acra, NY, NY; pashmina stole with pearl fringe, Bajra available through Sola, NY, NY; gloves, LaCrasia, NY, NY; formalwear, Lord West, Woodside, NY; flowers, Priscilla Schaefer, Glorimundi, NY, NY. **PAGE 190:** *top: left to right,* John Reilly, executive chef; Rachel John; Newton Pryce, pastry chef, Great Performances, NY, NY. *middle:* Toba Garrett, Cake Decorating by Toba, NY, NY; *bottom:* Priscilla Schaefer, Glorimundi, NY, NY. **PAGE 194:** pennants,

Pintura Studio, NY, NY; silver-sprayed green bamboo stakes, Smith & Hawken, San Francisco, CA: lanterns, Ikea, Elizabeth, NJ. **PAGE 195:** lanterns, Ikea, Elizabeth, NJ. **PAGE 196-197:** champagne bucket as finial, Service Party Rental, NY, NY; camellia branches, Priscilla Schaefer, Glorimundi, NY, NY; lanterns, Ikea, Elizabeth, NJ. **PAGE 198:** *left:* handprinted menu place cards, Heather Arak & Nathan Kanofsky, Arak-Kanofsky Studio, Easton, PA; calligraphy, Anna Pinto, Hoboken, NJ. *center:* tablecloth, napkin, Just Linens, NY, NY; dinner plate, Rosenthal, Carlstadt, NJ; sterling flatware, Reed & Barton, Taunton, MA; silversprayed skeletonized leaf, Loose Ends, Kreizer, OR; finger bowl, tumbler, Tampopo, San Francisco, CA; flowers, Glorimundi, NY, NY. *right:* vintage sterling lampshade; glass candlestick base, Dansk, Lenox Brands, Lawrenceville, NJ. **PAGE 199:** quilted tablecloth, napkins, Just Linens, NY, NY; tables, ballroom chairs, Service Party Rental, NY, NY; dinner plates, Rosenthal; sterling flatware, Reed & Barton, Taunton, MA; silver-sprayed skeletonized leaves, Loose Ends, Kreizer, OR; finger bowls, tumblers, Tampopo, San Francisco, CA; flowers, Glorimundi, NY, NY; can-

dles, Perin-Mowen, NY, NY; glass candlesticks, Dansk, Lenox Brands, Lawrenceville, NJ; sugar box, Gail Watson Cakes, NY, NY. **PAGE 200:** tables, chairs, Service Party Rental, NY, NY; linens, Just Linens, NY, NY. **PAGE 202:** *left:* shot glasses, Service Party Rental, NY, NY; silver-edged napkin, Dransfield & Ross, NY, NY. *center:* tumblers, Tampopo, San Francisco, NY, NY; sterling tray, Tudor Rose Antiques, NY, NY. *right:* silver coffeepots; Service Party Rental, NY, NY. **PAGE 203:** silver champagne buckets, Service Party Rental, NY, NY; champagne, Veuve Cliquot Demi-Sec, imported by Cliquot USA. **PAGE 204-205:** galvanized buckets, Ikea, Elizabeth, NJ; glassware, Arc International, Millville, NJ; White Star champagne by Moet-Chandon imported by Schieffelin and Somerset, NY, NY. **PAGE 206:** table, glassware, plates, coffeepots, Service Party Rental, NY, NY; linens, Just Linens, NY, NY; silver tray with handle, Towle Silversmiths, East Boston, MA; silver butler tray without handles, Wallace Silversmiths, East Boston, MA; sterling flatware, Reed & Barton, Taunton, MA; flowers, Glorimundi, NY, NY; large silver chalices, Carnevale, Memphis, TN ; silver mint julep cups, Kirk Stieff, Lenox Brands,

Lawrenceville, NJ. **PAGE 208:** *top*: foie gras hors d'oeuvres, Great Perfomances, NY, NY. *bottom*: brie croustade with caviar hors d'oeuvres, Great Performances; silver charger, Service Party Rental, NY, NY. **PAGE 209:** scallops with black truffles, Great Performances, NY, NY; porcelain plate, Service Party Rental, NY, NY. **PAGE 210:** *left*: kiwi granita served in a crystal sugar bowl, Great Performances, NY, NY; sterling plate, Tudor Rose Antiques, NY, NY. *right*: lobster risotto, Great Performances; porcelain bowl, Rosenthal, Carlstadt, NJ. **PAGE 211:** veal loin chops, Great Performances, NY, NY; porcelain plate, Rosenthal, Carlstadt, NJ. **PAGE 212:** souffle, tuile, Great Performances, NY, NY; souffle pot, Bridge Kitchen Supplies, NY, NY; silver plate, Service Party Rental, NY, NY. **PAGE 213:** meringue cones, Great Performances, NY, NY; silver tray, Gorham, Lenox Brands, Lawrenceville, NJ. **PAGE 214-215:** cake, Cake Decorating by Toba, NY, NY; silver tray, Towle Silversmiths, East Boston, MA; embroidered organza overlay, Just Linens, NY, NY; chalices, Carnevale, Memphis, TN; ballroom chairs, tables, Service Party Rental, NY, NY. **PAGE 216:** invitation design and printing, Heather Arak & Nathan Kanofsky,

Arak-Kanofsky Studio, Easton, PA; calligraphy, Anna Pinto, Hoboken, NJ. **PAGE 217:** hand-molded sugar boxes, Gail Watson Cakes, NY, NY; silvered almonds, Richart Design et Chocolates, NY, NY; ribbons, Offray & Son, Chester, NJ; embroidered tablecloth, Just Linens, NY, NY. **PAGE 218:** lavender candles, Perin-Mowen, NY, NY; glass candlesticks, Dansk, Lenox Brands, Lawrenceville, NJ. **PAGE 219:** iron candelabra, Simon & Company, Culver City, CA; candles, Perin-Mowen, NY, NY; shot glasses, table, Service Party Rental, NY, NY; tablecloth, Just Linens, NY, NY; flowers, Glorimundi, NY, NY. **PAGE 220:** *top to bottom*: flowers, antique Mexican silver chalices, Glorimundi, NY, NY. **PAGE 221:** bouquet, Glorimundi, NY, NY. **PAGE 222:** mercury-glass ornaments, East of Eden, Mt. Pleasant, SC. **PAGE 223:** *top*: assorted mercury-glass ornaments braided into garland, East of Eden, Mt. Pleasant, SC. *middle*: centerpiece, Glorimundi, NY, NY; glass compote, Abigails, Alexandria, LA; sugar boxes, Gail Watson Cakes, NY, NY. *bottom*: eucalyptus centerpiece, silver trumpet vase, Glorimundi, NY, NY; candlesticks, Dansk, Lenox Brands, Lawrenceville, NJ; candles, Perin-Mowen, NY, NY. **PAGE 224:** crystal prisms, Artifacts, Palestine,

TX; ribbons, Offray & Son, Chester, NJ. **PAGE 225:** camellia garland, Glorimundi, NY, NY; crystal prisms, Artifacts, Palestine, TX.

FAVORS

PAGE 226: handmade paper bags, Marie-Cleste Edwards, DH Productions, Paper Mill & Press, Kent Lakes, NY; tissue, Paper Access, NY, NY; calligraphy, Harriet Rose, NY, NY. **PAGE 228:** petit fours, Cheryl Kleinman Cakes, Brooklyn, NY; glassine envelopes, B & H Photo Supply, NY, NY; ribbon, Offray & Son; calligraphy, Stephannie Barba, NY, NY. **PAGE 229:** *top*: decorated almonds, Ricki Arno, Rosie's Creations, NY, NY. *bottom*: silver boxes, Hotel, Darien, CT; almonds, Daprano & Company, South San Francisco, CA. **PAGE 230:** *top*: lollipops, Hammonds Candies available at Li-Lac Chocolates, NY, NY; rubber stamps, Kate's Paperie, NY, NY; ribbons, Just Accents, NY, NY. *bottom*: Steven Klc, McLean, VA. **PAGE 231:** photo display water domes, One 2 Free Imports, El Monte, CA; calligraphy and illustration, Stephannie Barba, NY, NY. **PAGE 232:** sugar box, Gail Watson Cakes, NY, NY; ribbon, Vaban International, Atlanta, GA. **PAGE 233:** *top and bottom*: sugar favors, Betty Van Norstrand,

Poughkeepsie, NY. **PAGE 234:** *top*: porcelain hearts, Hooven & Hooven Porcelain, Berkeley, CA; calligraphy, Stephannie Barba, NY, NY. *bottom*: calligraphy, Stephannie Barba, NY, NY; organza ribbon, Midori, Seattle, WA. **PAGE 235:** Japanese sweet bean cakes, Toraya, NY, NY; calligraphy, Maria Thomas, Pendragon, Ink, Whitinsville, MA; ribbon, Mokuba, NY, NY.

PAGE 246: individual wedding cake, Cheryl Kleinman, Brooklyn, NY; serving dish, Ostafin Design, New York, NY. **PAGE 249:** calligraphy and illustration, Stephannie Barba, NY, NY. **PAGE 352:** crystal crown, Marlies Möler, Hamburg Germany; ring pillow, Angel Threads, Brooklyn, NY.

acknowledgments

T H I S   I S   T H E last page to be written and the one that gives me the most anxiety to draft. It's been just over two years since I first discussed my ideas for this project with my agent, Janis Donnaud. I am thankful for her wise council and encouragement. The past twenty-four months have been a whirlwind of planning sessions and photo shoots. Over 300 photos later, I have so many people to thank for helping me make this book a reality.

I am grateful to my editors, Joseph Montebello, who trusted my point of view and Megan Newman who enthusiastically embraced the book. Many thanks also to the dedicated staff at HarperCollins for all their efforts on my behalf.

I am indebted to Susi Oberhelman and her elegant sense of graphic design which made every page of this book sensational. I have also been blessed to work with an able partner, Siobhán McGowan, who polished my thoughts into perfect prose.

I am delighted to thank Ross Whitaker again. This book is our third effort together. Ross's glorious photos speak for themselves, but it was his friendship and sense of humor that made me look forward to our many, many days together. I thank Robert Bacall for repeatedly juggling Ross' calender to meet my photo schedule. Ross and I both thank Lali &

Inder Color Lab, especially Inder Mahendru, Sunder Raj Sura and Anand Ramchal, for the outstanding processing of our Kodak film. We thank Paul Schuts, Marcella Field, Rebecca Bennett, and Lorraine Pantic who made our shoots efficient and fun. And of course thanks to Ross' kids, Irene and Bill who were always so patient waiting for their Daddy to come home.

I thank all my talented friends— providers and industry specialists—who enthusiastically helped me animate my message. All are mentioned within the pages of this book. I thank their staffs and families who may go unnamed here but certainly not unappreciated. Once again, special thanks to Marcy Blum, Katie and Michael Meeks, Daniel Matroce, Rosemary Watson, Ann Gish, Lynn and Jim Gregerson, Zelda Tannenbaum, Patricia Bowden-Luccardi, Priscilla Schaefer, Toba Garrett, Liz Newmark, John Reilly, Newton Pryce, Rachel John, Todd Fiscus, Raegan B. McKinney, Susan Holland, Ed Magel, Ceasar Sanchez, Leonardo Iturregui, Kim De Paolera, Frank Marino of Black Tie Limo, Fran Diesu and Old Westbury Gardens, Jan Kish, Cheryl Kleinman, Margaret Braun, Peter Callahan, Beth Parker, Mark Dundon, Preston Bailey, Geoff Howell, Todd Moore, Rick Teale, Steven Klc, Kayo Der Sarkissian, Marie-Celeste Edwards, Stephannie Barba, Gail

Watson, Anna Pinto, Nancy Angel, Esther Smith, Dikko Faust, Heather Arak and Nathan Kanofsky, Caroline Paget Leake, Harriet Rose, Ricki Arno, Maria Thomas, Bernard Maisner, Linda Leiberman and Ira Siegel of Service Party Rentals, Polly Schoonmaker, Ellen Baumwoll, Betty van Norstrand, Christopher Bassett, Reem Acra, Amsale, Jonas and Ursula Hegeswisch, Erisa Yuki, Robert Danes, Edgardo Bonilla, Michelle Roth, Judith Luneau and the staff of the Stowehoff Inn, Stowe, Vermont and the staff of Everymay-on-the-Delaware, Erwinna, Pennsylvania; and Diana Shiel, Linda Meehan, Neysa Rojan, Josephine Dillon of the Silver Trust,

Love is a mysterious passion that fuels the wedding business and each of our lives in so many ways. The couples portrayed in this book are lucky benefactors of this delicious element; thankfully they let me document tender moments to illustrate my story. Thanks to Linette Dunbar and Grant Aumell who enjoyed many blessings this year; thanks to Magdalena Mickiewicz and Steven Benisty who ignore challenges of distance and treasure the time they share with each other; thanks to Regina Whitaker (a.k.a. Mrs. Ross Whitaker, who graciously shared her husband with me this year), Martina Gates and Tracy Trevett, girl-friends and moms with generous spirits; and

many, many thanks to Star, Michelle, Quincy, Brownen, Elisabeth, Betsy, Timothy and Hope Childs, who readily embraced the cause, opened their homes to our troops and made us all feel like family. I am so glad that one photo also memorializes Kotzebue Childs, the family dog whose happy spirit will be missed.

My office is a tiny place but it bustled with activity. I am indebted to my friends and co-workers: Machell Espejo, Magdalena Mickiewicz, Sujatha Raman, Juan Sebastin Aragon, Kimberly Evan, Maria Capatorto, Kerry Reardon, Maeve Yore, Heather O'Donnel, Carla Randau, Susan Holmes, Liz Schiable, Laura Leong, Debra Shapiro, Tracy Trevett and her AADA recruits and Audrey Razgaitis. This talented, energetic crew literally helped me survive.

I thank my many co-editors at Bride's Magazine for creating a beautiful world where readers can dream and where I am so happy to work.

And finally special thanks to Mom and Dad, my sister Tish and her husband Mike who were ready to lend a hand, a truck, a home. I thank my best friend and husband, Brett, who did double and triple duty while I was in the trenches. I also thank my children Ryan and Evan, who were always good sports and ready with needed hugs.

RESOURCES

LISTED HERE ARE MANY of my favorite wedding providers—the following vendors, artists, manufacturers, wholesalers and designers were handpicked for the quality of their work, their reliability, and their commitment to service. Those marked with an asterisk are featured in *The Perfect Wedding Reception*. If you're looking for more fashion and beauty sources pick up a copy of *The Perfect Wedding*.

A few rules of thumb will go a long way in making this planning period an easier one for you. Remember always that you are the customer. Don't hesitate to discuss your tastes, needs, and budget requirements; many establishments offer additional options and custom details on request and will go out of their way to accommodate your wishes. If you don't find what you're looking for close to home, consider contacting businesses located outside your area; some vendors will travel or ship products to meet your needs. And don't be shy about asking for referrals before buying or hiring—reliable businesses are proud of their work and will happily give you the names of previous clients. Lastly, be sure to get written contracts and sales receipts for major purchases and services, with all important details itemized.

Finally, I ask my readers and providers to help me keep this list up-to-date. Let me know when contact numbers change, if businesses close or if you are happy or unhappy with services provided. You can always contact me at mariamcbride.com. Congratulations and happy planning!

ALBUMS & JOURNALS

NAME	PHONE	ADDRESS	COMMENTS
Apiary Press	310.450.3681	Santa Monica, CA 90405	
Arch	415.433.2724	San Francisco, CA 94133	
Books by Hand	505.255.3534	Albuqerque, NM www.bookbinder.com	kits for albums
Cavallini & Co	800.226.5287	San Francisco, CA 94111	leather albums
Daisy Arts	310.396.8463	Venice, CA www.daisyarts.com	hand-tooled leather; call for local availability
D.H. Productions Papermill & Press*	888.343.4263	Kent Lakes, NY www.dhproduction.net	handmade paper photo boxes, totes
Flax	415.552.2355	San Francisco, CA 94103	
Gump's	415.982.1616	San Francisco, CA 94108	
It's a Wrap!	214.520.9727	Dallas, TX 75205	
Kate's Paperie*	212.941.9816	561 Broadway New York, NY 10012	handmade papers, albums, custom invitations
Klaus Rotzscher	510.845.3653	Berkeley, CA	
Kozo Arts	415.351.2114	San Francisco, CA www,kozoarts.com	decorative papers a specialty
Nina Sue Nusynowitz	212.691.2821	New York, NY www.crash.com/emb	etched aluminum, stainless albums
Oggetti	310.277.0889	Los Angeles, CA	
On Your Marque	415.543.6700	San Francisco, CA	custom albums, embossing
Pine Street Papery	415.332.0650	Sausalito, CA.	
Soolip Paperie	310.360.0545	West Hollywood, CA.	

R E S O

T. Anthony	212.750.9797	New York, NY	leather albums;
	800.722.2406	www.tanthony.com	catalog
Tiffany & Co.	212.755.8000	New York, NY	
	310.273.8880	Beverly Hills, CA	

ARCHIVAL SUPPLIES

NAME	PHONE	ADDRESS	COMMENTS
Gaylord Brothers	800.634.6307	Syracuse, NY	tissues, boxes; mail order acid-free products; catalogue
Lacis	510.843.7178	2982 Adeline St. Berkeley, CA 94703	
Light Impressions	800.828.6216	Rochester, NY www.lightimpressionsdirect.com	photo presentation
Photographic Archives	214.352.3167	5117 W. Lovers Lane Dallas, TX 75209	acid-free tissue, boxes
Talas, Inc.	212.219.0770	New York, NY	

ARTISANS

NAME	PHONE	ADDRESS	COMMENTS
Acme Sandblasting	212.477.1060	41 Great Jones Street New York, NY	sandblasting
American Wood Column Corporation	718.782.3163	913 Grand Street Brooklyn, NY	carved wood columns
Barbara Randa	215.322.8634	Richboro, PA	pumpkin carver
Betsy Krieg Salm	607.387.533.	Interlaken, NY www.betsykriegsalm.com	hand painted face screens

Bobbie Lefenfeld	413.528.6007	Great Barrington, MA	crystal lamp shades
Carla Weisberg	212.620.5276	New York, NY	custom textile design
Carriage House	800.669.8781	Brookline, MA	handmade papers
Coffin & King	480.970.1670 602.224.9869	Scottsdale, AZ	gilded decorative objects
David Rogers	212.830.4587	Glenwood Landing, NY	willow crafts
Dieu Donné Papermill	212.226.0573	433 Broome St. New York, NY 10013	handmade papers, custom watermarks
Exquisite Glass	212.674.7069	New York, NY	etching for decorative glass panels, mono-grammed glassware
G. Wolff Pottery	203.868.2858	New Preston, CT	horticultural earthenware
Gary Halsey	718.398.7521	Brooklyn, NY	decorative painter
Gay Merill Gross	212.645.5670	New York, NY www.oragami-usa.org	paper folder, origami author
Hoboken Pottery	201.659.8965	Hoboken, NJ.	handmade tiles
Home Portraits	914.682.3771	White Plains, NY www.susanstillman.com	portraits of homes, wedding locations
Ig Mata	212.979.7921	New York, NY www.igmata.com	photographs on glass, paper, cloth
Kim Kushner	415.388.4913	1001 Bridgeway, Ste. 560 Sausalito, CA 94965	custom gift wrap
K & Z Engraving	212.719.1137	45 West 47th Street New York, NY	engraves all metals
Lynn Rubino	212.807.7525	New York, NY	custom illustrations
Marc Musters*	212.243.0040	New York, NY	custom decorative objects
Miriam Kaye	413.296.4534	Chesterfield, MA	mosaics

R E S O

Nancy H. Strailey	814.238.5715	State College, PA	custom wedding fans
Pamela Hill	209.286.1217	Mokelumne Hill, CA	quilts
Patrick Clark	718.634.3397	Rockaway Park, NY	master glassman
Penn & Fletcher	212.239.6868	New York, NY	custom embroidery
Redstone Studios	914.666.7235	Millwood, NY	hand-painted canvas maps
Richard Jordan	212.255.4611	New York, NY	decorative painter
Smyers Glass	707.745.2614	Benicia, CA	handblown glassware
Stitchworks	212.255.2573	New York, NY	custom embroidery
Susan Eslick	415.255.2234	San Francisco, CA	custom ceramics
Teresa W. Chang	212.229.2292	New York, NY	ceramicist
Tom Penn	212.645.5213	Long Island City, NY	custom silversmith
Toshiko Tanaka	212.674.3768	New York, NY	hand emroidery
Wendy Lindkvist	415.381.3365	San Francisco, CA	custom stained glass
Yona Levine*	212.777.5260	New York, NY	crystal bead accessories
Zelda Tannenbaum*	718.217.4846	Hollis Hills, NY	paper maker, embossing

ART SUPPLIES

NAME	PHONE	ADDRESS	COMMENTS
Amsterdam Art	415.387.5354	San Francisco, CA	
Arch	415.433.2724	407 Jackson St. San Francisco, CA 94111	
Asel Art Supply	817.335.8168	Fort Worth, TX	

Baggot Leaf Company	212.431.4653	430 Broome St. New York, NY 10013	gold leaf supplies
The Bead Store	212.628.4383	1065 Lexington Ave. New York, NY 10021	
Bemiss - Jason Corp.	800.544.0093	Neenah, WI www.beemiss-jason.com	craft supplies
Binders Discount Art Center	214.739.2281	9820 North Central Expwy. Dallas, TX 75231	custom framing
The Caning Shop	800.544.3373	Berkley, CA www.caning.com	rattan poles, craft tools, rawhide lacing
Eastern Glass	201.847.0001	Wyckoff, NJ	glass etching supplies
Flax Art & Design	800.547.7778	1699 Market St. San Francisco, CA 94103	
Hygloss Products	800.444.9456	Wallington, NJ www.hygloss.com	
Lee's Art Shop	212.247.0110	220 W. 57th St. New York, NY 10019	
Metalliferous	212.944.0909	New York, NY www.metaliliferous.com	metallic supplies and tools
Mill Valley Art Materials, Inc.	415.388.5642	433 Miller Ave. Mill Valley, CA 94941	
New York Central Art Supply	800.950.6111	New York, NY www.nycentralart.com	catalog, specialty papers
Pearl Paint	212.431.7932	308 Canal St. New York, NY 10013	
Rubberstilzkin	510.440.9406	44384 S. Grimmer Blvd. Fremont, CA 94537	decorative rubber stamps
Sam Flax	212.620.3010	New York, NY	
Sax Arts & Crafts	414.264.1580 800.558.6696	New Berlin, WI	fine Japanese lace papers
Sepp Leaf	800.971.7377 212.683.2840	New York, NY	metallic leaf, supplies, tools and classes

R   E   S   O

BAKING SUPPLIES

NAME	PHONE	ADDRESS	COMMENTS
August Thompson	800.645.7170	Glen Cove, NY	utensils
Broadway Panhandler	212.966.3434	477 Broome St. New York, NY 10013	bakeware
Cake Art Supplies	415.456.7773	San Rafael, CA	
Country Kitchen	630.969.2624 219.482.4835	3225 Wells Street Fort Wayne, IN 46808	cake and candy supplies
Gloria's Cake and Candy Supplies	630.969.2624 310.391.4557	Los Angeles, CA www.gloriascakecandy suplys.com	cookie presses; mail-order catalog
House on the Hill	630.969.2624	Villa Park, IL	cookie presses
La Cuisine, The Cooks's Resource	800.521.1176 703.836.4435	Alexandria, VA www.lacuisineus.com	professional baking equipment
New York Cake & Baking	800.942.2539 212.675.2253	56 W. 22nd St. New York, NY 10011	variety gum paste flowers, doilies, baking supplies
Parrish's Cake Decorating Supplies	310.324.CAKE 800.736.8443	225 West 146th Street Gardena, CA 90248	mail order
Sugar Bouquets	973.538.3542 800.203.0629	Morristown, NJ	decorative molds
Sugar 'n Spice	415.387.1722	Daly City, CA	
Williams-Sonoma	800.541.2233	San Francisco, CA	baking, kitchen supplies

BEAUTY

NAME	PHONE	ADDRESS	COMMENTS
Patricia Bowden-Luccardi*	203.324-1463	Stamford, CT	freelance stylist for winter and fall chapters
Kim DePaolera*	973.942.4927	Totowa, NJ	freelance stylist for spring chapter
Rick Teal*	212.206.0901	New York, NY	freelance stylist for summer chapter

BOOKBINDERS/BOX MAKERS

NAME	PHONE	ADDRESS	COMMENTS
Angela Scott	516.537.3918	Sag Harbor, NY	
Barbara Mauriello	201.420.6613	Hoboken, NJt	frames, books and boxes
Campbell-Logan Book Bindery	800.942.6224 612.332.1313	Minneapolis, MN www.campbell-logan.com	
Carolyn Chadwick	212.727.8842	New York, NY	leather albums, a specialty
Center for Book Arts	212.460.9768	New York, NY	referrals, classes
Henry Nuss Bookbinder	214.747.5545	2701 Main St. Dallas, TX 75226	
Judy Ivry	212.677.1015	New York, NY	custom-made albums
Marjorie Salik	212.219.0770	New York, NY	by appointment
M.C. Edwards	888.343.4263	Kent Lakes, NY	wedding photo boxes
Tactile Books	212.242.4320 206.784.6063	New York, NY Seattle, WA	folder frames

RESO

Talas	212.219.0770	New York, NY www.talasonline.com	wedding photo boxes
Trade Bindery	415.981.1856	San Francisco, CA	
Yesteryear	310.278.2008	West Hollywood, CA	

BRIDAL REGISTRY

NAME	PHONE	ADDRESS	COMMENTS
ABC Carpet & Home*	212.473.3000	888 Broadway New York, NY 10003 www.abchome.com	home accessories, furniture, linens, tableware
The Accent Shop	317.844.5112	1520 E. 86th St. Indianapolis, IN 46240	
Asprey & Garrard	212.688.1811	New York, NY	sterling
Baccarat	212.826.4100	New York, NY	crystal
Bardith Ltd.	212.737.3775	New York, NY	porcelain
Barneys New York	800.777.0087 212.826.8900	Beverly Hills, CA, New York, NY www.barneys.com	
Bed Bath & Beyond	800.GOBEYOND 212.255.3550	620 Sixth Avenue New York, NY 10011 www.bedbathandbeyond.com	call for local availability
Bergdorf Goodman	212.753.7300	New York, NY	
Bloomingdale's	888.2.wed	New York, NY www.bloomingdales.com	
Calvin Klein Home*	877.256.7373 212.292.9000	New York, NY	

China Silver & Crystal Shop	206.441.8906 800.759.5817	2809 Second Ave. Seattle, WA 98121	
Christofle Silver	212.683.4616 800.799.6886	New York, NY www.christofle.com	silversmiths
Collections	317.283.5251	Indianapolis, IN	
Crate & Barrel	800.967.6696	Chicago, Il www.crateandbarrel.com	housewares, tableware
David Orgell	310.273.6660	Beverly Hills, CA	
Durr	612.925.9146	Edina, MN	home furnishings
Domain	425.450.9900	Bellevue, WA	housewares
Earthly Possessions	617.696.2440	Milton, MA	tableware
Felissimo	800.565.6785 212.247.5656	New York, NY www.felissmo.com	gifts
Fishs Eddy	212.420.9020	889 Broadway New York, NY 10003	restaurant ware
Fortunoff	800.777.2807 516.832.9000	1300 Old Country Rd. Westbury, NY 11590 www.fortunoff.com	full-service registry
Geary's	310.273.4741	351 N. Beverly Dr. Beverly Hills, CA 90210	
Georg Jensen	800.546.5253 312.642.9160	New York, NY Chicago, IL	sterling
Gump's*	800.444.0450 415.984.9341	San Francisco, CA www.gumps.com	china, crystal, decorative accessories
Hechts	202.628.6661	Washington, DC	
Hollyhock	213.931.3400	Los Angeles, CA.	

R   E   S   O

The Home Depot	800.654.1914		call for local outlet
Lenox	800.635.3669	New Jersey	china
L.L. Bean	800.341.4341	Freeport, ME	sporting, camping goods
Macy's	212.994.3800 800.701.7112	New York, NY California	
Maison Moderne	212.691.9603.	New York, NY	
Marshall Field's	312.781.3545	Chicago, IL	
Matsu	617.266.9707	Boston, MA	tableware
Michael C. Fina	800.289.3462	New York, NY www.michaelcfina.com	cystal, china, sterling
Mxyplyzyk*	212.989.4300	New York, NY www.mxyplyzyk.com	
Neiman Marcus	310.550.5900	Beverly Hills, CA	
Paragon Sporting Goods	212.255.8036	867 Broadway New York, NY 10003	
Pavillon Christofle	310.858.8058	Beverly Hills, CA	sterling
Portico Soho	888.259.8598	New York, NY www.porticonewyork.com	linens
Pottery Barn	800.922.5507	www.pottery barn.com	housewares, tableware
Replacements	800.replace	Greensboro, NC	hard-to-find china
Room Service	214.369.7666	4354 Lovers Lane Dallas, TX 75225	decorative accessories, vintage furnishings
Room with a View	310.453.7009	Santa Monica, CA	
Royal Copenhagen	212.759.6457	New York, NY	

Silver Vault	214.357.7115	Dallas, TX	
Something Wonderful	317.848.6992	9700 Lakeshore Dr. E. Indianapolis, IN 46280	
Stanley Korshak	214.871.3600 800.972.5959	Dallas, TX	
Steuben	800.424.4240	New York, NY	fine crystal
Tabletop Designs	631.283.1313	Southampton, NY. www.stephaniequeller.com	
Takashimaya	800.753.2038	693 Fifth Ave. New York, NY 10022	tableware, decorative accessories
Target		www.target.com	affordabale style
Tiffany & Co.	212.755.8000	New York, NY	sterling, crystal, china
Tower Records	212.799.2500	New York, NY	music registry
Troy	212.941.4777	138 Greene St. New York, NY 10012	contemporary home furnishings
Waterford Wedgwood	800.677.7860	New York, NY	china, crystal
TheWedding Channel.com		www.weddingchannel.com	on-line registry
Wedding List	212.988.6166 011715841222	New York, NY London, England www.theweddinglist.com	registry service
William-Wayne*	212.288.9243	New York, NY	decorative accessories
Zona	212.925.6750	New York, NY	artisan crafts

R   E   S   O

CAKE TOPPERS

NAME	PHONE	ADDRESS	COMMENTS
Arturo Diaz	214.760.8707	Dallas, TX	custom sugar paste figurines
Cory Lewis	305.296.9323	Key West, FL	custom marzipan figurines
Gia Grosso	212.627.7827	New York, NY	paper doll cut-outs; cookie figurines
If Girls Ruled The World	510.237.8726	Richmond, CA	porcelain figurines
It Figures	818.509.0200	Studio City, CA www.itfiuresonline.com	custom porcelain figurines
Laura Wilensky	914.338.2199	Kingston, NY	porcelain figurines
Perfect Couple	212.255.4841	New York, NY	multi ethnic figurines a specialty
Party Block	800.205.6400	College Station, TX www.thepartyblock.com	multi ethnic figurines, accessories
Rebecca Russell	212.255.7530	New York, NY	marzipan figurines

CALLIGRAPHY

NAME	PHONE	ADDRESS	COMMENTS
Alan Simon	317.257.6968	Indianapolis, IN	by hand or computer
Anna Pinto*	201.656.7402	Hoboken, NJ	contemporary hand lettering, design
Barbara Callow	415.928.3303	San Francisco, CA	
Bernard Maisner*	732.899.9858 212.899.9858	Bayhead, NJ	hand lettering

Carole Maurer	610.642.9726	Wynnewood, PA	
Caroline Paget Leake*	718.486.6044	Brooklyn, NY	copperplate specialist
Calligraphic Arts	214.522.4731	Dallas, TX	
The Calligraphy Company	201.866.1985	Secaucus, NJ	multilingual
Calligraphy Studios	212.964.6007	New York, NY	multilingual
Cheryl Jacobsen	319.351.6603	Iowa City, IO	
Claire Mendelson	416.784.1426	Toronto, Ontario	ketubah artist
Cyberscribes		cyberscribes@onelist.com	
Eleanor Winters	718.855.7964	Brooklyn, NY	copperplate specialist
Evelyn Schramm	214.969.2823	Dallas, TX	
Goldy Tobin	425.454.6143	Seattle, WA	
Jay Greenspan	212.496.5399	New York, NY	ketubah artist, illuminator
Jonathan Kremer	610.664.9625	Narberth, PA	medieval lettering
Janet Redstone	312.944.6624 800.484.7919	Chicago, IL	custom monograms
K2 Design	214.522.2344	Dallas, TX	
Kevin Karl	817.926.2888	Fort Worth, TX	
Margie Reed	206.232.7343	Seattle, WA	
Papineau	510.339.2301	Oakland, CA	

R   E   S   O

Pendragon Ink *	508.234.6843	Whitinsville, MA	
Richard Jordan	212.255.4511	New York, NY	Carolingian script
Special Letters	310.316.1533	Redondo Beach, CA	
Stephannie Barba *	212.592.8919	New York, NY stephanniebarba@hotmail.com	
The Elegant Pen	914.368.0673	Suffern, NY elegantpenlori@yahoo.com	
Toni Elling	888.827.6477 518.827.6477	Middleburgh, NY	
Washington Calligapher's Guild	301.897.8637	Merrifield, VA	references

CANDLES

NAME	PHONE	ADDRESS	COMMENTS
American Pie	415.929.8025	3101 Sacramento St. San Francisco, CA 94115	
Barker Co.	800.543.0601	Seattle, WA	candlemaking supplies
Beeskep II *	518.761.5578	Johnstown, NY	molded candles
Candelier	415.989.8600	60 Maiden Lane San Francisco, CA 94108	
The Candle Shop *	212.989.0148	118 Christopher St. New York, NY 10014	
The Candlestick	800.972.6777	38 West Spain St. Sonoma, CA 95476	
Creative Candles *	16.474.9711	Kansas City, MO www.craftedcandle.com	all lengths, all colors

Dadant & Sons	800.637.7468	Hamilton, IL	candle-making supplies
Fantastico	415.982.0680	539 Sixth St. San Francisco, CA 94103	
Fillamento	415.931.2224	2185 Fillmore St. San Francisco, CA 94115	
General Wax & Candle Company	818.765.6357	N. Hollywood, CA www.genwax.com	
Hurd Beeswax Candles	707.963.7211 800.977.7211	3020 Saint Helena Hwy. N. Saint Helena, CA 94574	candle factory
Ilume	213.782.0342	8302 W. Third St. Los Angeles, CA 90048	candle emporium
Knorr Beeswax Products	619.755.3430 800.807.bees	14906 Via De La Valle Delmar, CA 92014	
Lamplight Farms	414.781.9590 800.645.5267	4900 N. Lilly Rd. Menomonee Falls, WI 53051	wax candles, oil lamps
The Market	817.334.0330	3433 W. Seventh St. Fort Worth, TX 76107	
Nelson Candles	800.323.5901 602.944.1926	Phoenix, AZ	floating rose candles
Perin-Mowen*	212.219.3937 214.748.2128	New York, NY Dallas, TX	hand-rolled beeswax candles
Point a al Ligne	877.321.0020	San Francisco, CA www.pointalaligne.com	
Pourette Candle	206.789.3188	Seattle, WA www.pourette.com	
Sample House & Candle Shop	214.599.0335 817.429.7857	Dallas, TX Fort Worth, TX	
Summer House	415.383.6695	21 Throckmorton Ave. Mill Valley, CA 94941	

R E S O

Visual Design	205.345.9992	Tuscaloosa, AL	candle bracelets
Wicks & Sticks	281.874.0800 888.55.WICKS	Houston, TX www.wicksnsticks.com	large chain store, call for local outlets

CATERERS

NAME	PHONE	ADDRESS	COMMENTS
A Mano Catering	781.444.2132	Needham, MA	
Affairs to Remember	404.872.7859 404.876.6314	Atlanta, GA	
A Joy Wallace Catering Production	305.252.0020	Miami, FL	
All in Good Taste	412.321.5516	Pittsburgh, PA	
Along Came Mary	213.931.9082	Los Angeles, CA	
Ann Walker Catering	415.460.9885	Corte Madera, CA	
Another Roadside Attraction	901.525.2624	Memphis, TN	
Apple Spice	801.359.8821	Salt Lake City, UT	
Atrium Catering	612.339.8322	Minneapolis, MN	
Betty Zlatchin Catering	415.641.8599	San Francisco, CA	
Bread & Butter	310.390.9662	Culver City, CA	
Cafiero Lussier	212.352.2958	New York, NY	
Calihan Gotoff Catering	312.587.3553	Chicago, IL	

Callahan Catering*	212.327.1144 610.583.7500	New York, NY Folcroft. PA	caterer: summer chapter
Capers Catering	781.648.0900	Arlington, MA	
The Catered Affair	781.982.9333	Hingham, MA	
The Catering Co.	816.444.8372	Kansas City, MO	
Catering St. Louis	314.961.7588	St. Louis, MO	
Cathy's Rum Cake	602.945.9205	Scottsdale, AZ	
Chardonnay's	904.730.8081	Jacksonville, FL	
Chow! Catering	405.752.9991	Oklahoma City, OK	
The Comfort Diner	212.867.4555	New York, NY.	
The Common Plea	412.281.5140	Pittsburgh, PA	
Creative Edge	212.741.3000	New York, NY	
Creative Gourmets	617.783.5555	Boston, MA.	
Crystal Catering	317.615.1500	Indianapolis, IN	
Design Cuisine	703.979.9400	Arlington, VA	
DM Cuisine Ltd.*	212.673.5348	New York, NY	caterer: fall chapter
Duck-Duck Mousse	310.392.4956	Santa Monica, CA	
Elaine Bell Catering	707.996.5226	Sonoma, CA www.elainebellcatering	
Entertainment Caterers	617.262.2605	Boston, MA	
Epicurean Catering	303.770.0877	Greenwood Village, CO	

R   E   S   O

Events by Steven Duvall	843.763.9222	Charleston, SC	
Fascinating Foods	901.276.3555	Memphis, TN	
Feastivities	817.377.3011	Fort Worth, TX	
Ferree Florsheim	773.282.6100	Chicago, IL	
Food Art	504.524.2381	New Orleans, LA	
Food Company	214.939.9270	Dallas, TX	
Food for All Seasons	734.747.9099	Ann Arbor, MI	
Food in Bloom	205.223.6819	Portland, OR	
Food in Motion	212.766.4400	New York, NY	
Gai Klass	310.559.6777	Culver City, CA	
Gracious Catering	414.786.1030	Wauwatosa, WI	
Great Performances*	212.727.2424	New York, NY	caterer: winter chapter
Heck's	216.464.8020	Cleveland, OH	
J.G. Melons	415.331.0888	Sausalito, CA	
Jack Norman	414.425.4720	Franklin, WI	
Joel's Grand Cuisine	800.335.8994	New Orleans, LA	
Kates Fine Catering	615.298.5644	Nashville, TN	
Katherine's Catering	734.930.4270	Ann Arbor, MI	
La Bocca Fina	510.264.0276	Hayward, CA	
La Pêche	502.451.0377	Louisville, KY	

Le Petit Gourmet	303.388.5791	Denver, CO
Lee Epting Catering	770.641.1825 770.641.7772	Roswell, GA
Lewis Steven's Distinctive Catering	602.991.2799	Scottsdale, AZ
Magazzini-Latour	011.6.6.319284	Rome, Italy
Marian's Island-Wide Catering	808.621.6758	Wahiawa, HI
McCall Associates	415.552.8550	San Francisco, CA
Michel Richard	310.275.5707	Los Angeles, CA
Mitchell Cobey	312.397.0090	Chicago, IL
Mood Food	212.243.4245	New York, NY
Moveable Feast	734.663.3278	Ann Arbor, MI
Now We're Cooking	415.255.6355	San Francisco, CA
Panache Catering	303.790.2648	Englewood, CO
Partysist Caterers	504.488.4234	New Orleans, LA
Paula LeDuc	510.547.7825	Emeryville, CA
Pavilion Catering	414.671.2001	Milwaukee, WI
Poulet	510.845.5932	Berkeley, CA
The Prairie Star	505.867.3327	Bernalillo, NM
Proof of the Pudding	404.892.2359	Atlanta, GA
Ritz Charles	317.846.9158	Carmel, IN

R E S O

Robbins Wolfe	212.924.6500	New York, NY	
The Roostertail Catering Club	313.822.1234	Detroit, MI	
The Ruins	206.285.7846	Seattle, WA	
Ruth Meric	713.522.1448	Houston, TX	
Saffron 59	212.253.1343	New York, NY	
Sammy's	216.523.5899	Cleveland, OH	
Sargeant's Inc.	615.373.9331	Brentwood, TN	
Simply with Style	508.228.6248	Nantucket, MA	
Someone's in the Kitchen	505.986.8077	Santa Fe, NM	
Somerset	310.204.4000	Los Angeles, CA	
Sonny Bryan's Smokehouse	214.353.0027	Dallas, TX	
South City Kitchen	404.873.7358	Atlanta, GA	
Susan Gage	301.839.6900	Oxon Hill, MD	
Susan Holland & Company*	212.807.8892	New York, NY	caterer: spring chapter
Susan Mason Inc.	912.233.9737	Savannah, GA	
Taste Catering	415.550.6464	San Francisco, CA	
Taste of Scandinavia	651.482.8876	North Oaks, MN	
Tavola Catering	503.225.9727	Portland, OR	
Thomas Caterers	317.542.8333	Indianapolis, IN	
Thomas Preti Caterers	212.764.3188	Long Island City, NY	

Thymes Two	415.921.1673	San Francisco, CA www.thymes two. com
Tiger Rose Catering	415.388.3287	Mill Valley, CA
Tony's At Home	713.622.6779	Houston, TX
Upper Crust Inc.	502.456.4144	Louisville, KY
Vivande	415.346.4430	San Francisco, CA
Walter Burke	505.473.9600	Santa Fe, NM
Wendy Krispin	214.748.5559	Dallas, TX
West Coast Productions	714.953.4368	Santa Ana, CA

CONFECTIONERS

NAME	PHONE	ADDRESS	COMMENTS
Black Hound	212.979.9505 800.344.4417	New York, NY www.blackhoundny.com	fine cookies
Candy Conversation Hearts	800.725.6763	ww.bridallink.com	
Chocolates by Bernard Callebaut	800.526.6553	ww.bernardchocolate.com	
Crills Saltwater Taffy	805.772.1679 805.772.2615	Morro Bay, CA www.crills.qpg.com	
Daprano & Co.	650.588.5418	South S.F., CA www.daprano	jordan almonds chocolates
de Granvelle	800.9.BELGIUM	New York, NY 212.953.8888 www.degranvelle.com	Belgian chocolatier

RESO

Doughnut Planet	212.505.3700	New York, NY	doughnuts
Economy Candy	800.352.4544 212.254.1832	New York, NY ww.economycandy.com	old-fashioned candies kosher items
Eleni's Cookies	212.255.7990	New York, NY	iced sugar cookies
Elk Candy Co.	212.585.2303	New York, NY	marzipan a specialty
English Cottage Candies	717.866.4789	Myerstown, PA	chocolate heart shaped boxes
F.J. Pastries,	212.541.5858	New York, NY	petits fours
French Sweet Gourmet	011.331.56.337.620	Paris, France www.frenchsweetgourmet.com	traditional French confections
Gia Grosso	212.627.7827 917.226.0869	New York, NY	custom cake toppers, cookies
The Gift Factory	818.365.6619 800.284.2422	Sylmar, CA	
Godiva Chocolatier	800.9.GODIVA	New York, NY www.godiva.com	
Hammond Candies	88.226.3999	Denver, CO	lollipops
Haute Chocolature	212.751.9591	New York, NY	custom work
JLH European Trading	415.626.3672	San Francisco, CA	imported chocolates
Johnson Candy	617.776.6255	www.johnsoncandy.com	cystallized heart candies
Kim Juarado*	718.932.4838	Astoria, NY	marzipan
La Maison du Chocolat	800.988.5632	New York, NY www.lamaisonduchocolat.com	
Laura's Candies	330.966.3866	N. Canton, OH www.laurascandy.com	candy, nuts, ice cream

Li-Lac Chocolates	800.624.4874 212.242.7374	New York, NY	
Luisa Chocolatier	949.582.5867	Laguna Hills, CA	wedding favors
Meadowsweets	888.827.6477	Middleburgh, NY	crystallized flowers
Minamoto Kiochoen*	212.489.3747	New York, NY	Japanese candies
Monaco Baking Company	562.906.8683 800.569.4640	Sante Fe Springs, CA www.monacobaking.com	custom design iced cookies
Monastery of the Angels	323.466.2186	Los Angeles, CA	hand-made chocolates
Moravian Cookie Shop	800.537.5374 336.924.1278	Winston-Salem, NC www.moraviancookie.com	heart-shaped spice cookies
Neuhaus Chocolate Shop	516.883.7400 ext. 10	Port Washington, NY	imported and handmade chocolates
Nutcracher Sweet	412.963.7951	Pittsburgh, PA	sugar place cards
Oh Sew Sweet.	800.550.3112 219.659.1279	Whiting, IN www.ohsewsweetinc.com	chocolate favor heart boxes a specialty
Richart Design et Chocolates	800.742.4278	New York, NY	Parisian chocolates, silk-screen patterns
Rosie's Creations*	212.362.6069	New York, NY	iced cookies, almonds
Special Orders	212.722.0486	New York, NY	decorated mints, cubes
Tea and Cake Confections	212.645.2742	Ridgefield Park, NJ www.teaandcake.com	lollipops in a variety of natural flavors
Teuscher Chocolates of Switzerland	212.751.8482	620 Fifth Ave. New York, NY 10020	
The Sweet Factory	312.432.3239 800.333.3629	New York, NY www.fanniemaycandies.com	

R   E   S   O

The Sweet Life	212.598.0092	New York, NY	traditional sweets
Tom and Sally's Handmade Chocolates	800.827.0800 802.254.4200	Brattleboro, VT www.tomandsallys.com	novelty Belgian chocolates
The Truffle Mistress	212.780.9771	New York, NY	homemade truffles
Toraya	212.861.1700	New York, NY	traditional Japanese confectionery
Umanoff & Parsons	212.219.2240	New York, NY	kosher desserts

CONSULTANTS & EVENT PLANNERS

NAME	PHONE	ADDRESS	COMMENTS
Aloha Weddings	808.254.6449	Kailua, HI	
Along Came Mary	213.931.9082	Los Angeles, CA	
An Event to Remember	516.593.4164	Long Island City, NY	
Apples & Oranges	707.254.8980	Napa, CA	
Barabara Tyler	401.885.9598	East Greenwich, RI	
Bruce Southworth	847.695.6070	Highland Park, IL	
Candy Langan	203.454.1585	Weston, CT	
Celebrations	901.525.5223	Memphis, TN	
Connie Kerns	510.339.3370	San Francisco, CA	
Creative Parties	301.654.9292	Bethesda, MD	

Elegant Affairs	212.533.4771	New York, NY	
Elegant Occasions	212.704.0048 973.361.9200 888.361.9177	New York, NY Denville, NJ elegwed204@aol.com	
Event of the Year	212.570.1055	New York, NY	
Frankie Berger Events	310.820.2255	Los Angeles, CA	
Gale Sliger	214.637.5566	Dallas, TX	
Gary Barvard	317.687.1920	Indianapolis, IN	
Geoff Howell Studio*	212.366.0567	New York, NY	custom sets & decorative visuals for summer chapter
Grand Luxe	201.327.2333	Allendale, NJ	European weddings
Great Performances	212.727.2424	New York, NY	caterer: winter chapter
Harriet Rose Katz	212.535.0005	New York, NY www.gourmetadvisory.com	
Hopple Popple	617.964.6550	Newton, MA	
Jacque Designs	310.859.6424	Beverly Hills, CA	
Judith Schwartz	212.570.9818	New York, NY	
Kate Edmonds	212.366.4447	New York, NY	
Leopold Productions	212.388.2511	New York, NY	
Linda Alpert	847.831.9891	Highland Park, IL	
Lori Draper	406.961.5580	Victor, MT	
Lynn Schlereth	973.379.5627	Short Hills, NJ	

R   E   S   O

Marcy Blum Associates*	212.688.3057	New York, NY	author "Weddings for Dummies"
Margo Bouanchaud	225.952.9010	Baton Rouge, LA	
Marsha Heckman	415.388.2295	Mill Valley, CA	
McCall Associates	415.552.8550	San Francisco, CA	
Michelle Lally	412.731.2028	Pittsburgh, PA	
Nina Austin	214.871.3634	Dallas, TX	gown consultant and event planner
Parties, Parties	415.331.0544	Sausalito, CA	
Party Concepts	310.820.2255	Los Angeles, CA	
Pefect Parties	212.563.2040	New York, NY	
Peter Callahan *	212.327.1144	New York, NY	caterer: summer chapter
Premier Parties	914.273.4779	Armonk, NY	
Preston Bailey Designs*	212.691.6777	New York, NY	florals: summer chapter
Princeton Event Consultants	609.683.4467	Princeton, NJ www.princetonevent consult.com	
Saved by the Bell	212.874.5457	New York, NY	
Society Weddings	914.371.4517	Hillcrest, NY www.societyweddings.com	
Stanlee Gatti	415.558.8884	San Francisco, CA	
Susan Dorenter	201.768.6663	Demarest, NJ	invitation designer and event planner

Name	Phone	Address	Comments
Susan Holland & Company,*	212.807.8892	New York, NY www.susanholland.com	caterer: spring chapter
Tie the Knot	650.968.2564	Mountain View, CA	
Todd Moore*	212.989.9088	New York, NY	linens: summer chapter
Tom Thomas	212.253.0009	New York, NY	corporate event specialist
Two Design Group*	214.741.3145	Dallas, TX	florals: spring chapter
Watson & Company*	415.441.5251	San Francisco, CA	
The Wedding Resource	415.928.8621	San Francisco, CA	

DECORATIVE ACCESSORIES

NAME	PHONE	ADDRESS	COMMENTS
Albuhi*	404.220.3496	Atlanta, GA www.members.xoom.com/ albuhi	polished aluminum
Aluminum Pottery	610.995.2950	Wayne, PA www.reallifegoods.com	
America	609.397.6966	Lambertville, NJ www.americadesigns.com	decorative arts, antiques
Angèle Parlange Design*	504.897.6511	New Orleans, LA	tableware and linens
Annie J*	212.741.0112	New York, NY	pillows, tabletop
Amy Perlin Antiques	212.593.5756	New York, NY	
Anthropologie*	212.343.7070	New York, NY www.anthropologie.com	objects from around the world

R E S O

Annie's Treasures	800.872.6888	S. San Francisco, CA	glass votives, fruit baskets
Artifacts*	800.678.4178 903.729.4178	Palestine, TX www.artifactsinc.com	glass prisms
Argentum- The Leopard's Head	415.296.7757	San Francisco, CA	antique silver
Art Matters Catalog	800.979.2787	New York, NY	decorative objects by mail
B & B International*	888.818.2713	New York, NY www.bbint.net	metal chairs, silver objects
Beall & Bell	631.477.8239 631.477.5062	18 South Street Greenport, NY 11944	vintage Americana
Billie Beads	718.372.3954	Brooklyn, NY	vintage collectibles
Bountiful	310.450.3620	Venice, CA	vintage collectibles, linens
Brian Windsor Art	212.274.0411	New York, NY	garden objects
Brooks Barrel Co.	800.398.2766 410.228.0790	Cambridge, MD www.brooksbarrel.com	pine barrels; metal hoops, catalog
The Brown Bag	415.922.0390	San Francisco, CA	giftwrap, gifts, novelties
Burts Cason*	888.641.6859 225.383.6859	Baton Rouge, LA	glazed pottery
Canterbury Woodworks Inc.*	603.783.9511	Canterbury, NH	Shaker-style trays, boxes; catalog
Charles William Gaylord Antiques	415.392.6085	San Francisco, CA	
Chista*	212.924.0394	New York, NY www.chista.net	teak furniture llighting
C.I.T.E. Design*	212.431.7272	New York, NY	
Cobweb	212.505-1558	New York, NY	imported antiques

Country Originals	601.366.4229 800.249.4229	Jackson, MS	iron furniture
David Landis Design	212.563.7568	New York, NY www.davidlandisdesign.com	candlestick bobeches
De vera	415.788.0828	San Francisco, CA	
Design via Carioca*	415.642.9321	San Francisco, CA	cast-aluminum pots, garden furniture
Dorian Webb*	212.684.5544	New York, NY	Venetian glass
East of Eden*	800.914.7737 843.856.9668	Wando. SC	glass ornaments
Ecologia*	908.996.3255	Little York, NJ	sea glass nuggets
Elizabeth Meredith	707.763.1532	Petaluma, CA	miniature light strings
Elizabeth Street	212.644.6969 212.941.4800	New York, NY www.elizabethstreetgallery.com	garden ornaments
Eli Wilner	212. 744.6521	New York, NY www.eliwilner.com	period frames, reproductions
Emdee International*	404.614.0409	Atlanta, GA www.goemdee.com	chenile throws, runners
Ercole	718.797.4270	Brooklyn, NY	mosaic accessories
Fillamento	415.931.2224	San Francisco, CA	objects for table, home and entertaining
Folly	212.925.5012	New York, NY	antique garden accessories
Forrest Jones	415.567.2483	San Francisco, CA	glassware
Gallery Japonesque	415.391.8860	San Francisco, CA	Japanese antiques, dishware, ceramics
The Gardener	510.548.4545	Berkeley, CA	unusual containers, hand- made paper, ceramics
Garden Antiquary	212.757.3008 914.737.6054	Cortland Manor, NY	

RESO

Gargoyles	215.629.1700	Philadelphia, PA www.gargoylesltd.com	vintage props
Geoff Howell*	212.366.0567	220 W. 19th St. New York, NY 10011	custom decorative objects, illustrations, visuals: summer chapter
George Dell Inc.	212.206.8460	New York, NY	glassware, metalware
Gill & Lagodich*	212.619.0631	New York, NY	period frames
Great American Collective	415.922.2660	San Francisco, CA	antiques
Handcraft of South Texas	800.443.1688	Pharr, TX	wire containers; custom design available
Hen-feathers	610.277.0800 800.282.1910	King of Prussia, PA www.hen-feathers.com	decorative fiberglass containers; planters
Heritage Antique Maps	215.340.9662	Doylestown, PA www.heritageantiquemaps.com	maps from 15th – 20th century
Homestead	800.679.0729 830.997.5551	Fredricksburg, TX	rural Americana
Ikea*	800.434.4532	Elizabeth, NJ www.ikea.com	contemporary decorative accessories
Interieur Perdu	415.543.1616	San Francisco, CA www.interieurperdu.com	bistro chairs
Interieurs	212.343.0800	New York, NY www.interieurs.earthlink.com	provincial furniture
John Derian Company	212.677.3917	New York, NY	decoupage glass plates French imports
Jo Liza International	818.252.1082	Sun Valley, CA www.jo-liza.com	imported hammered tin mirrors
Kashmir*	212.861.6464	New York, NY	Indian and Oriental textiles, containers
Kinsman Company	800.733.4146	Point Pleasant, PA	garden accessories, wire chandelier baskets

Kiybele Creations	914.273.6659	Armonk, NY	garden accessories
La Maison Moderne*	212.691.9603	New York, NY 10011	gift registry
Leekan Designs	212.226.7226	New York, NY	Asian and Middle East decorative accessories
Lunares*	415.621.0764	San Francisco, CA	aluminum accessories
Mango Leaf	212.889.9198	New York, NY www.mangoleaf.com	natural woven boxes
The Maine Bucket Co. Inc	800.231.7072 207.784.6700	Lewiston, ME ww.mainebucket.com	pine buckets and barrels
Meryl Waitz	212.675.7224	New York, NY	pewter frames, gifts
Metal Urges	310.578.6710	Santa Monica, CA	candelabras, iron objects
The Mews	214.748.9070	Dallas, TX	antiques, furniture, sterling, candlesticks, linen
Michelle Columbine	415.927.8884	Corte Madera, CA	
Monticello Studio	773.227.4540	Chicago, IL	plaster columns, sconces
Morgik Co. Inc.	800.354.5252 212.463.0304	New York, NY www.morgik.com	wrought iron to order
Mozayiks	212.219.1160	285 Mott St. New York, NY 10012	mosaic objects, custom huppah poles
Munder-Skiles	212.717.0150	New York, NY	garden ornaments
Naomi's Antiques To Go	415.775.1207	San Francisco, CA.	American pottery
Niedermaier	212.966.8631	New York, NY	
Oi	415.282.3695 415.333.5271	San Francisco, CA www.oipeach.com	velvet and organza flower bouquets
Olde Good Things*	888.551.7333 212.989.8401	124 West 24th Street New York, NY 10011	architectural antiques reclaimed hardware
Oriental Gifts	212.608.6670	96 Bayard Street New York, NY 10013	Oriental imports

R E S O

Pacific Circle Arts	510.540.1233	1049 Folger Street Berkeley, CA 94710	rattan and grass baskets, Indonesian handicrafts
Pandora's Plasterworks	212.627.1578	153 Prince Street New York, NY 10012	plaster casts to paint and gild
Parisé	800.375.3572	Nashville, TN	votives, linens, place cards
The Pavilion Antiques	415.459.2002	San Anselmo, CA	country American, European antiques
Peter Patout Antiques	504.522.0582	New Orleans, LA www.peterpatouantiques.com	classic American and European furniture
Phoenix Imports	212.608.6670	New York, NY	paper lanterns, sandal- wood fans
Pine St. Papery	415.332.0650	Sausalito, CA	paper goods a specialty
Props, Displays & Interiors, Inc.*	212.620.3840	New York, NY	plaster columns custom woodshop
R. H.	415.346.1460	San Francisco, CA	garden and home accessories
Rayon Vert	415.861.3516	San Francisco, CA	tabletop accessories
Rose Tattoo	305.293.1941	Key West, FL	gold-leafed containers
Room Service	214.369.7666	Dallas, TX	home accessories, vintage finds
Russell Johnson Imports	310.280.1001	Beverley Hills, CA artthang.com	old-fashioned seltzer bottles
Rustica*	212.965.0004	63 Crosby New York, NY 10012	Southeast Asian accessories
Sahara Moroccan Imports*	212.462.2645	New York, NY	lanterns, chairs, screens, glassware
Santa Monica Antique Market	310.314.4899	1607 Lincoln Blvd. Santa Monica, CA 90404	antiques and collectibles
Sea Shell City	888.743.5524	Fenwick Island, DE	shells, nautical artifacts
Seibert & Rice	973.467.8266	Short Hills, NJ	terra cotta containers

Shaker Workshops	800.840.9121 508.827.9900	Ashburnhan, MA www.shakerworkshops.com	classic Shaker boxes and furniture
Sue Fisher King	415.922.7276	3067 Sacramento St. San Francisco, CA 94115	ceramics, linens, toiletries; gifts for the house
Sugar & Spice	415.387.1722	Daly City, CA	
Summer House	415.383.6695	21 Throckmorton Ave. Mill Valley, CA 94941	candles, jewelry, furniture, gifts for the house
Tail of the Yak	510.841.9891	2632 Ashby Ave. Berkeley, CA 94705	decorative objects, linens, candles
The Loom Company*	212.366.7215	26 West 17th Street, #701 New York, NY 10011	artists' representative, by appointment
Tinman*	914.265.2903	75 Main Street. Cold Spring, NY 10516	vintage Americana
Treillage*	212.535.2288	418 E. 75th St. New York, NY 10021	garden ornaments
Urban Archaeology	212.431.6969	285 Lafayette St. New York, NY 10012	garden accessories
Vanderbilt & Co.	707.963.1010	1429 Main St. St. Helena, CA 94574	baskets, French linens

ETHNIC ARTIFACTS

NAME	PHONE	ADDRESS	COMMENTS
Aid to Artisans	860.677.1649	Farmington, CT www.aid2artisans.org	not-for-profit source of global handcrafts
A Thosand Cranes	212.233.4439	New York, NY	origami ornaments
Allen & Cowley & Home*	800.279.1634	Phoenix, AZ www.allen-cowley.com	Mexican wedding cookies
Beads of Paradise	212.620.0642	New York, NY	African artifacts

R E S O

Gallery Japonesque	415.391.8860	824 Montgomery Street San Francisco, CA	Japanese ceramics
Hoshoni	212.674.3120	309 East 9th Street New York, NY	Native American objects
Irish Secret	212.334.6711	155 Spring Street New York, NY	Irish handicrafts
J. Levine Books & Judaica	800.553.9474 212.695.6888	New York, NY www.levinejudaica.com	huppas, catalog
Katagiri & Company	212.755.3566	224 East 59th Street New York, NY 10022	Japanese provisions, tableware
Kinnu	212.334.4775	New York, NY	Indian handicrafts
Lee Carter's Tzin Tzun Tzan	415.641.0373	San Francisco, CA www.leecartercompany.com	Mexican folk art
Mostly Bali	212.777.9049	324 East 9th Street New York, NY 10003	Pacific-rim artifacts
Old Japan	212.633.0922	382 Bleecker Street New York, NY	traditional Japanese accessories
Peace Craft Company	877.291.3566 617.623.375	Somerville, MA	origami ornaments
Pearl River Mart	212.431.4770	New York, NY	Oriental imports
Sahara Moroccan Imports*	212.462.2645	New York, NY	
Surma	212.473-3550	New York, NY	Ukrainian folk art
Tesoros Trading Company	800.926.6812 512.479.8341	Austin, TX www.tesoros.com	Latin American folk art
Things Japanese	212.371.4661 617.623.3756	127 East 60th Street New York, NY	Japanese decorative accessories
Tibet Collection	800.318.5857	Washington, DC www.dZi.com	talismans, prayer flags
White Buffalo Lodges	406.222.7390	Livingston, MT www.avicom.net/whitebuffalo	tipis, shelters, wagon covers

FABRICS & NOTIONS

NAME	PHONE	ADDRESS	COMMENTS
B & J Fabrics, Inc	212.354.8150	263 West 40th Street New York, NY 10018	fine apparel fabrics
Beckenstein Home Fabrics	212.366.5142	4 West 20th Street New York, NY 10011	
Britex Fabrics	415.392.2910	San Francisco, CA . www.britexfabrics.com	vintage buttons, ribbons, lace
Calico Corners	415.461.0923	Greenbrae, CA	
Diamond	213.931.8148	611 S. La Brea Ave. Los Angeles, CA 90036	
Edley Associates	800.TRICOTS 516.334.7700	Jericho, NY www.wedley.com	pre-cut tulle circles, spools, flocked tulle
Fabric Center	508.343.4402	Fitchburg, MA	
Gardner's Ribbons & Lace	817.640.1436	2235 E. Division Arlington, TX 76011	buttons, beads, trims, vintage too
Heaven on La Brea	213.965.8200	Los Angeles, CA	vintage fabrics
Heirloom Woven Labels	609.722.1618	Moorestown, NJ www.members.aol.com /heirloom	custom fabric labels
Interior Alternatives	800.988.7775 302.454.3232	1325 Coochs Bridge Rd. Newark, DE 19713 www.decoratewaverly.com	silk fabrics
International Silks & Woolens	213.653.6453	8347 Beverly Blvd. Los Angeles, CA 90048	
Jo-ann	615.771.7676	Frankli, TN www.joann.com	
Lacis	510.843.7178	2982 Adeline St. Berkeley, CA 94703	
Lilac Bow Yoke	510.548.5448	Berkley, CA	buttons

M & J Trimming	212.391.9072	New York, NY www.mandjtrimmings.com	notions, custom millinery
Poppy Fabrics	510.655.5151	Oakland, CA	
Promenade Fabrics	504.522.1488	New Orleans, LA	ribbons, fabrics
Richard Brooks Couture Fabrics	214.739.2772	6131 Luther Lane Dallas, TX 75225	
Rose Brand	800.223.1624	New York, NY www.rosebrand.com	theatrical fabrics
Satin Moon Fabrics	415.668.1623	32 Clement St. San Francisco, CA 94118	
Sheru	212.730.0766	49 W. 38th St. New York, NY 10018	notions, beads
Silk Surplus	212.753.6511	235 E. 58th St. New York, NY 10022	designer fabrics for slipcovers
Tessuti International	212.221.5780	228 W. 39th St. New York, NY 10018	silk tulle
Tinsel Trading	212.730.1030	47 West 38th Street New York, NY	vintage flowers braiding, trims

FASHION, FORMALWEAR & ACCESSORIES

NAME	PHONE	ADDRESS	COMMENTS
Alan Flusser	212.888.7100	New York, NY	custom formalwear
Alecca Carrano	800.356.9559	New York, NY	embroidered shawls
Amsale*	212.583.1700	New York, NY	bridal salon
Amy Jo Gladstone	718.899.8010	Long Island City, NY	boudoir slippers, silk shoes

Angel Threads*	718.246.0551	Brooklyn, NY www.angelthreadsnyc.com	bridal accessories; mail-order catalog
Anne Fontaine*	212.343.3154	93 Greene Street New York, NY 10012 www.annefontaine.com	all white shirts, blouses
Badgley Mischka	212.921.1585	New York, NY	call for local availability
Barneys New York	310.276.4400	Beverly Hills, CA	
Bergdorf Goodman	212.753.7300	New York, NY	bridal salon
Bridal Boutique of Manhasset	516.869.8455	1681 Northern Blvd. Manhasset, NY 11030	
Stanley Korshak	214.871.3611	Dallas, TX	bridal salon, wedding consultant
Peggy Barnes	713.622.2298	Houston, TX	bridal salon
Carrott & Gibbs	303.449.2821	Boulder, CO	silk bow ties for men
Capezio Dance	212.245.2130	New York, NY	ballet slippers
Chic Parisien	305.448.5756	Coral Gables, FL	bridal salon
Kenneth Cole	800.KEN.COLE	New York, NY	shoe salon
Cole-Haan*	212.765.9747	New York, NY	shoe salon
Edgardo Bonilla	877.BONILLA	Haddonfield, NJ	bridal designer, ring bearer pillows a specialty
Eve France Designs	212.727.9020	New York, NY	metallic mesh
Gene Meyer*	212.980.0110	New York, NY	silk ties for men
The Hat Shop	212.219.1445	New York, NY	stocks Lola Millinery
Henri Bendel	212.247.1100	New York, NY	
Daytons	612.375.2162	Minneapolis, MN	bridal salon
Exclusives	312.664.8870	Chicago, IL	bridal salon
For the Bride	913.381.1060	Prairie Village, KS	bridal salon

R   E   S   O

Jim Hjelm Occasions	212.764.6960	New York, NY	attendant collection
The House of Broel	504.522.2220	New Orleans, LA	bridal salon
Josephine Sasso	212.396.9692	New York, NY	attendant collection
Kleinfeld	718.833.1100	Brooklyn, NY	bridal salon
La Crasia*	212.594.2223	New York, NY www.weglove.com	gloves
Les Habitudes	310.273.2883	Los Angeles, CA	
Lippincott*	888.902.5584 908.237.0400	Ringoes, NJ	deluxe parasols, canes, shawls
Lisa Shaub	212.675.9701	New York, NY	custom millinery
Lord West*	800.275.9684	Woodside, NY	mens' formalwear
Malatesta*		malatex@spacelab.net	sarongs
Manolo Blahnik	212.582.3007	New York, NY	shoe salon
Manolo Collection	212.997.4697	New York, NY	contemporary bridal
Marlies Möller	011404480945	Hamburg, Germany	crystal crowns
Maria V. Pinto	312.360.1330	Chicago, IL	stoles
Marina Killery	212.924.5660	New York, NY	custom millinery
Marina Morrison*	415.984.9360	San Francisco, CA	bridal salon
Marshall Field's	312.781.3545	Chicago, IL	bridal salon
Mary Ann Maxwell	713.529.3939	Houston, TX	bridal salon
Meg Cohen Design	212.473.4002	New York, NY	cashmere stoles
Mespo Umbrellas	718.680.3601	Brooklyn, NY	oversized cottons
Michelle Roth	212.245.3390	New York, NY	bridal salon
Miller's Harness	212.673.1400	New York, NY www.millerharness.com	oilcloth duster coats

Neill Bieff	121.278.0054	New York, NY	couture collection
Neiman Marcus	713.621.7100 312.642.5900	Houston, TX Chicago, IL	
N. Peal*	800.962.5541	New York, NY	cashmere
Nicole Miller	310.652.1629 415.398.3111	West Hollywood, CA San Francisco, CA	attendant collection
Norma Kamali	212.957.9797	New York, NY	
Pamela Dennis	212.354.2100	New York, NY	call for local availability
Paris Hats & Veils	513.948.8888	Cincinnati, OH	crown
Patrick Cox	212.759.3910	New York, NY	shoe salon
Paul Smith	212.627.9770	New York, NY	menswear
Rachel Puckett	203.972.8530	New Canaan, CT	wedding gown stylist
Prairie New York	212-391-6600	New York, NY	shawls, wraps, sarongs
Priscilla,	617.267.9070	Boston, MA	bridal salon
Rados Protic*	212.431.3218	New York, NY	crystal crowns
Reem Acra*	212.414.0980	New York, NY	custom couture gowns
Richard Tyler	213.624.9299	Los Angeles, CA	custom bridal
Robert Danes	212.941.5680	New York, NY	
Sandra Johnson*	310.247.8206	Los Angeles, CA	bridal couture
Shaneen Huxham	212.944.6110	New York, NY	handmade gloves
Sigerson/ Morrison	212.219.3893	New York, NY	shoe salon
Sola	212-620-0988	New York, NY sola@telcocom.com	pashmina shawls
Stephane Lessant	201.792.0208	Hoboken, NJ	bridal couture

RESO

Stuart Weitzman	212.750.2555	New York, NY	shoe salon
Suky Rosan	610.649.3686	Ardmore, PA	bridal salon
Swarovski*	212.213.9001	New York, NY	fine Austrian crystal
Sylvia Heisal	212.719.3916	New York, NY www.sylviaheisal.com	designer dresses
The Ultimate Bride	312.337.6300	Chicago, IL	
Tia Mazza	212.989.4349	New York, NY	crowns and veils
Vanessa Noel Couture	212.333.7882 508.228.6030	New York, NY Nantucket, MA www.vanessanoel.com	shoe salon
Vera Wang Bridal	212.628.3400	New York, NY	
Watters & Watters	214.991.6994	Dallas, TX	attendants' gowns
The Wedding Dress at Saks Fifth Avenue	212.940.4288 404.261.7234	New York, NY Atlanta, GA	bridal salon
Wearkstatt*	212.334.9494	New York, NY	bridal salon
Worth & Worth	212.867.6058	New York, NY	hats for men
Yolanda	781.899.6470	Waltham, MA	bridal salon
Yumi Katsura	212.772.3760 212.772.2951	New York, NY www.yumikatsura.com	bridal salon
Zazu & Violets	510.845.1409	Berkeley, CA	made-to-measure straw hats

FAVORS & PACKAGING

NAME	PHONE	ADDRESS	COMMENTS
Almond Blossom	8212.362.4840	New York, NY	custom favors
Anne-Stuart Hamilton	203.778.9849	Ridgefield, CT	custom keepsakes
Apec	800.221.9403	900 Broadway New York, NY 10010	glassine envelopes, all sizes, colors
Canon's	302.738.3321	Newark, DE	favor boxes
Cazenovia Abroad	800.722.4327	Cazemovia, NY www.cazenoviagifts.com	sterling gifts, tussy-mussies
Consolidated Plastics	800.362.1000		kraft shopping bags
Create a Camera	800.410.8008	www.bestcameras.com	disposable wedding camera, custom packaging
Dana Krieg	888.893.6782	Mountain View, CA	custom gifts
Deborah Shapiro	212.532.2420	New York, NY	custom gifts
Forget Me Knots	415.921.0838	San Francisco, CA	bridesmaid favors
Grandma's Cupboard	330.784.1712	1297 Krumroy Road Akron, OH 44306	favor boxes
Hooven & Hooven*	510.486.1952	Berkeley, CA	porcelain ornaments
Ilene Chazenof	212.254.5564	New York, NY	vintage sterling
Joneses International*	800.566.3770	Walnut Creek, CA	woven baskets and mesh bags
Magical Beginnings Butterfly Farm	888.639.9995	New York, NY www.butterflyevents.com	monarch butterflies to release
Martha's Vineyard Candlemakers	508.693.9800	Vineyard Haven, MA www.candles.vineyard.net	mini beeswax wedding cake favors
Mod.Pac	800.666.3722	Buffalo, NY www.modpac.com	folding boxes for favors

R E S O

Mecca	626.577.0012	Pasadena, CA www.meccamecca.com	special event planning gift gallery
Nat Sherman	800.221.4330	New York, NY	cigars, accessories
One-2-Free Import Co.*	626.350.1171	El Monte, CA	photo insert snow domes
Restoration Hardware	415.924.8919	San Francisco, CA	reproduction gadgets, toys
Royal Lace	800.66.7692 203.847.8500	Norwalk, CT www.theroyalstore.com	doilies, paper goods
RTR Packaging	212.620.0011	27 West 20th Street New York, NY 10011	customizable shopping bags, boxes
Spectrum Ascona	800.356.1473	Bellingham, WA www.asconapkgcom	gourmet food packaging
Stoneworks	800.stone.61	Tuxedo, NY	engraved stones
Surprise Packages	800.711.3650	Norristown, PA www.surprisepackages.com	decorative gift boxes
Things Remembered	800.274.7367	www.thingsremembered.com	engravable gifts
US Can*	800.436.6830 410.686.6363	Baltimore, MD www.uscanco.com	lidded tin containers
Wired Up	201.947.8625	Fort Lee, NJ	by appointment

FLORAL DESIGNERS

NAME	PHONE	ADDRESS	COMMENTS
Andrew Pascoe	516.922.9561	Oyster Bay, NY	
Anthony Garden	212.737.3303	New York, NY	
Arrangement	305.576.9922	Miami, FL	
The Aspen Branch	800.707.3791 970.925.3791	Aspen, CO www.aspenbranchflorals.com	

Ateliér A Work Shop	214.750.7622	Dallas, TX	
Avant-Gardens	305.554.4300	Miami, FL	
Baumgarten Krueger	414.276.2382	Milwaukee, WI	
Blong Florists	904.389.7661	Jacksonville, FL	
Bloom	212.620.5666	New York, NY	event space to rent
Bloomers	415.563.3266	San Francisco, CA	
Blossoms	248.644.4411	Birmingham, MI	
Blue Meadow Flowers	212.979.8618	New York, NY	
Bomarzo	415.771.9111	San Francisco, CA	
Botanica	901.274.5767	937 S. Cooper St. Memphis, TN 38104	architectural and naturalistic garden styles
Botanicals on the Park	800.848.7674	St. Louis, MO	
Bouquets	303.333.5500	Denver, CO	
Brady's Floral Design	602.945.8776 800.782.6508	Scottsdale, AZ	
Carole Brunet	973.746.4465	Montclair, NJ	
Castle & Pierpont	212.570.1284	New York, NY www.castlepierpont.com	
Charles Radcliff	713.522.9100	Houston, TX	
Charleston Florist	843.577.5691	Charleston, SC	
Christian Tortu	011.33.1.55.42.65.15	6 Carrefour de L'Odeon Paris France 75006 www.takashimaya.com	
Christopher Bassett*	212.568.5091	New York, NY	

R E S O

Christopher Whanger	214.559.3432	Dallas, TX
Claire W. Webber	800.261.8605	Oakland, CA
Cornucopia	212.594.8944	New York, NY www.cornucopiaflowers.com
Country Gardens	216.333.3763	Cleveland, OH
Covent Gardens	513.232.4422	Mt. Washington, OH
The Crest of Fine Flowers	888.401.9856	Wilmette, IL
Curtis Godwin	910.484.4547	Fayetteville, NC
Cynthia's Creations	303.841.5381	Aurora, CO
Cynthia's Floral Designs	800.944.8246 904.398.5824	Jacksonville, FL
D'Clements	303.399.5543	Denver, CO
David Beahm	212.279.1344	New York, NY
David Brown Florist	713.861.4048	Houston, TX
Del Apgar	513.321.2600	Cincinnati, OH
Designs by Jodi	847.816.6661	Lake Bluff, IL
Devorah Nussenbaum et Verdure	510.548.7764	Berkeley, CA
Donald Vanderbrook	216.371.0164	Cleveland, OH
Ed Libby	201.666.7776	Westwood, NJ
Elizabeth House	704.342.3919	Charlotte, NC
Elizabeth Ryan	212 .995.1111	New York, NY

Emilia's Floral	801.943.7301	Draper, UT	
Enflora	317.634.3434	Indianapolis, IN	
English Garden	615.352.0094	Nashville, TN	
Esprit De Fleur	206.533.9277	Seattle, WA	
Fioridella	415.775.4065	San Francisco, CA	
Fujikami Florist, Inc.	808.537.9948	Honolulu, HI	
Fiori	612.623.1153	Minneapolis, MN	
Florals of Waterford*	201.327.0337	Saddle River, NJ www.waterfordgardens.com	florist: fall chapter
The Flower Studio	414.228.9200	Milwaukee, WI	
Flowers on the Square	817.429.2888	Fort Worth, TX	
Fred Palmer Flowers	505.820.0044	Santa Fe, NM	
Friendly Flower Gallery	919.596.8747	Durham, NC	
Garden Center	801.595.6622	Salt Lake City, UT	
The Garden Gate	800.646.5840	Dallas, TX	
Glorimundi	212.727.7090	New York, NY	florist: winter chapter
Hastings & Hastings	415.381.1272	Mill Valley, CA	
Heffernan Morgan	773.782.0800	Chicago, IL	
Hepatica	412.241.3900	Pittsburgh, PA	
Hibiscus	816.891.0808	Kansas City, MO	
Hilo Airport Flowers	808.935.8275	Hilo, HI	Hawaiian leis
Holliday's Flowers,	901.753.2400	Germantown, TN	

Incline Florist	800.556.5033	Incline Village, NV
Jacob Maarse	818.449.0246	Pasadena, CA
Jennifer Houser	516.537.5532 212.532.8676	Sag Harbor, NY New York, NY
Jerry Rose Flowers & Events	800.342.4490 973.762.1085*	Maplewood, NJ
Kate Stanley Design	415.227.4547	San Francisco, CA
Larkspur	612.332.2140	Minneapolis, MN
Larkspur	212.619.4055	New York, NY
Laurels Custom	213.655.3466	Los Angeles, CA
L. Becker Flowers	212.439.6001	New York, NY
Leslie Palme	718.622.6995	Brooklyn, NY
Living Creations	801.485.3219	Snowbird, UT
Lord & Mar	847.295.5456	Lake Forest, IL
Magnolias	502.585.4602	Louisville, KY
Main Street	415.485.2996	San Anselmo, CA
Marsha Heckman	415.388.2295	Mill Valley, CA
Martha A. Meier	203.259.4179	Southport, CT
Mary Ware	415.388.6323	San Francisco, CA
Michael Haley Ltd.	904.387.3000	Jacksonville, FL
Michaele Thunen	510.527.5279	Berkeley, CA
Miho Kosuda	212.922.9122	New York, NY
Mitch's Flowers	504.899.4843	4843 Magazine St. New Orleans, LA 70115

Nanz & Kraft Florist	502.897.6551	Louisville, KY	
Nature's Daughter	908.221.0258	Basking Ridge, NJ	
Newberry Brother's	303.322.0443	Denver, CO	
Palmer-Kelly	317.923.9903	Indianapolis, IN	
Perfect Presentations	504.522.7442	New Orleans, LA	
Peter A. Chopin Florist, Inc.	504.891.4455	New Orleans, LA	
Potted Gardens	212.255.4797	New York, NY	
Preston Bailey*	212.691.6777	New York, NY	florist: summer chapter
Prudence Designs	212.691.1356	New York, NY	
Regalo Flowers	505.983.4900	Santa Fe, NM	
Robert Bozzini	415.351.2823	San Francisco, CA	
Ron Wendt	212.290.2428	New York, NY	
Rosewood Florists	803.256.8351	Columbia, SC	
Russell Glenn	214.742.3001	Dallas, TX	
Ryan Gainey & Co.	404.233.2050	Atlanta, GA	
Salutations Ink	303.371.2393	Denver, CO	
Seasons	212.369.4000	New York, NY	
Silver Birches	626.796.1431	Pasadena, CA	
Spruce	212.414.0588	New York, NY www.spruceup.com	
Stacey Daniels Flowers	800.463.7632 914.762.8372	Ossining, NY	
Stanlee R. Gatti	415.558.8884	San Francisco, CA	
Stone Kelly	212.875.0500	New York, NY	

R E S O

Surroundings Flowers	800.567.7007 212.580.8982	New York, NY www.surroundingsflowers.com	
Suzanne Codi	202.269.4259	Washington, DC	
Ten Pennies	215.336.3557	Philadelphia, PA	
TFS	310.274.8491	Los Angeles, CA	
Thran's Flowers	702.588.1661	Stateline, NV	
Tim Condron	412.361.4057	Pittsburgh, PA	
Tommy Luke	503.228.3131	Portland, OR	
Tom Thompson	734.665.4222	Ann Arbor, MI	
Trochta's Flowers	800.232.7307	Oklahoma City, OK	
The Tulip Tree	615.352.1466	Nashville, TN	
Two Design Group*	214.741.3145	Dallas, TX	florist: spring chapter
Uptown Flowers	504.899.2923	New Orleans, LA	
Velvet Garden	323.852.1766	Los Angeles, CA	
Vines	505.820.7770	Santa Fe, NM	
Vollan Blumen	503.236.1713	Portland, OR	
VSF	212.206.7236	New York, NY	
Wayside Garden	812.945.3596	New Albany, IN	
Wells Flowers	317.872.4267	Indianapolis, IN	
Whitegate	213.465.1222	Los Angeles, CA	
Wildflowers of Louisville	502.584.3412	Louisville, KY	
Window Box	212.686.5382	New York, NY	gardens a specialty
Winston Florist	617.541.1100	Boston, MA	
Wisteria Design	612.332.0633	Minneapolis, MN	

The Woods	310.826.0711	Los Angeles, CA	
Xylem	412.967.9844	Pittsburgh, PA	
Zen Floral Design	214.741.4001	Dallas, TX	
Zezé Flowers	212.753.7767	New York, NY	

FLORAL & GARDEN SUPPLIES

NAME	PHONE	ADDRESS	COMMENTS
American Designer Pottery	888.388.0319	Dallas, TX www.amdesignerpottery.com	terra cotta urns
Archetique Enterprises, Inc.	212.563.8003	New York, NY	fiberglass and rustic containers
Ballard Designs	404.351.5099	Atlanta, GA	garden accessories by mail
The Baywoods	631.726.5950	Watermill, NY	garden accessories
B & J Supplies	212.564.6086	New York, NY	
Central Floral	212.686.7952	New York, NY	tools and suplies
Coast Wholesale	415.781.3034	San Francisco, CA	
Coco & Co.	214.748.1899	Dallas, TX	
Copper Arts	703.335.6060	Manassas, VA	metal pails
Country House	508.475.8463	Andover, MA	catalog
D. Blümchen & Company,	201.652.5595	Ridgewood, NJ	Victorian bouquet holders; catalog
Dorothy Biddle	570.226.3239	Greeley, PA	professional floral supplies by mail

Dulken & Derrick	212.929.3614	New York, NY www.dulkenandderrick.com	handmade flowers, silk, a specialty
Everyday Gardener	601.981.0273	Jackson, MS	
Foliage Garden	212.989.3089	New York, NY	flowering plants, trees; to buy or rent
Frank W. Manker	800.906.ROSE 516.289.5294	Patchogue, NY	wholesale roses
Fresh Oregon Holly	800.821.0172	St. Helens, OR	fresh-cut holly by mail
G. Wolff Pottery	203.868.2858	New Preston, CT	handthrown earthenware
The Galveston Wreath Company	409.765.8597	Galveston, TX	dried botanicals, berries, flowers
Gardener's Eden	800.822.9600	San Francisco, CA	catalog
Gary Page Wholesale Flowers	212.741.8928	New York, NY www.gpage.com	wholesale imported flowers
Grassroots Garden	212.226.2662	New York, NY	plants, trees
Green Valley Growers	707.823.5583	San Francisco, CA	wholesale floral farm
Kervar	212.564.2525	New York, NY	floral tape, oasis, ribbons
Kinsman	215.297.5613	River Road Point Pleasant, PA	garden and floral supplies by mail
Lady Slipper Designs	800.950.5903 218.751.0763	Bemidji, MN www.ladyslipperdesigns.com	birdhouses and birdfeeders
Lins International	800.423.9206 562.407.0616	Cerritos, CA www.linsinternational.com	silk flowers, foliage, garlands
Marders the Landscape Store	631.537.3700	Bridgehampton, NY	
The Marketplace	212.594.8289	New York, NY	columns, arbors for rent
Mecox Gardens	800.487.4854 631.287.5015	South Hampton, NY	

Metalcrafts	703.335.6060	Manassas, VA	copper containers, metal pails, vases
Moskatel's	800.562.5654 213.689.4830	Los Angeles, CA www.michaels.com	party, craft and floral supplies
Nature's Pressed	800.850.2499 801.225.1169	Orem, UT www.naturespressed.com	pressed flowers; catalog
New England Garden Ornaments	508.867.4474	North Brookfield, MA	garden structures; catalog
Oak Grove Mills	908.782.9618	Pittstown, NJ	flowering plants
OKS Flowers	212.268.7231	New York, NY	dried flowers, fruits, berries
Oregon Wire Products Co.	800.458.8344 503.255.5155	Portland, OR	wire frames for wreaths, topiaries
Pany	212.645.9526	New York, NY	artificial flowers
Paxton Gate	415.824.1872	San Francisco, CA	tools
Planter Resource	212.206.POTS	New York, NY	containers
Poor Richard's	212.297.5666	Point Pleasant, PA	
Princess Flowers	212.229.2088	New York, NY www.dried-flowers.com	dried flower products, whimsical flower dolls
Quentin Natural Materials	409.258.5744	Dayton, TX	dried local berries, grasses
Rosedale Nursery	914.769.1300	Hawthorne, NY	
Schoepfer Natural Artifacts*	718.389.8873	Long Island City, NY	preserved butterflies
Sein Import	212.675.0580	New York, NY	artificial flowers
Simple Pleasures	401.331.4120	Providence, RI	floral and garden supplies
Smith & Hawken*	800.776.3336 212.925.0687	New York, NY www.smithandhawken.com	catalog
Tancredi & Morgan	831.625.4477	Carmel, CA	imported gardenware

R E S O

Trimbles	631.734.6494	Cutchoque, NY	nursery
Waterford Gardens	201.327.0721	Saddle River, NJ www.waterfordgardens.com	water lillies
Well Sweep Herb Farm	908.852.5390	Port Murray, NJ 07865	herb plants, perennials

FOOD BANKS

NAME	PHONE	ADDRESS	COMMENTS
City Harvest	917.351.8777	New York, NY. www.cityharvest.org	food redistribution agency
Second Harvest National Foodbank Network	312.263.2303	Chicago, IL	national foodbank referral list

INFORMATION SOURCES

NAME	PHONE	ADDRESS	COMMENTS
American Institute for Conservation	202.452.9545	Washington, DC	list of historic sites
American Rental Association	800.334.2177	Moline, IL	national referral service; party rental brochures
Association for Bridal Consultants	203.355.0164	200 Chestnut Road New Milford, CT 06776	referral list of registered members
Flower Council of Holland	516.621.3625	Glenwood Landing, NY	call for local availability
Hagstom Map & Travel Center	212.398.1222	57 West 43rd Street New York, NY 10036 www.hagstrommaps.com	

The Knot		New York, NY www.theknot.com	on-line source guide
National Center for Health Statistics	301.458.4636	Hyattsville, MD www.cdc.goc	national data & info wedding licenses
National Limousine Association	800.NLA.7007	Lexington, KY	referral service; call for local availability
Neighborhood Cleaners Association	212.967.3002	New York, NY	referral service; call for local specialist
Roses, Inc.	517.339.9544	Haslett, MI	rose care info
Silver Trust International*	212.949.7050	New York, NY www.silverinfo.com	sterling gift guides
Society for Calligraphy	213.931.6146	Los Angeles, CA	call for referrals or instruction
Teleflora	310.231.9199	Los Angeles, CA.	florist referrals
Washington Calligraphers Guild	301.897.8637	Merrifield, VA	call for referrals
The Wedding Library	212.327.0100	New York, NY www.weddinglibrary.net	research boutique

LINENS

NAME	PHONE	ADDRESS	COMMENTS
ABH Design	212.688.3764	New York, NY	
Alma Slade Designs	800.367.9193 203.367.9193	61 Hurd Avenue Bridgeport, CT 06604	curtain sheers for tents and huppas
Alphapuck Designs	212.267.2561	139 Fulton Street, #210 New York, NY 10038	custom fabrications
Anichini	800.553.5309 802.889.9430	Turnbridge, VT	fine Italian linens

R E S O

Ann Gish*	805.498.4447	Newbury Park, CA	fine linens, silks
Ballroom Elegance	305.936.0669	Miami, FL	rentals only
Carla Weisburg*	212.620.5276	New York, NY	custom textile design, table linens, pillows
Covered Affairs	516.623.9012	Freeport, NY	custom table linens, rentals
Current	206.622.2433	1201 Western Seattle, WA 98101	linens; registry
The Curtain Exchange	508.897.2444	3947 Magazine Street New Orleans, LA 70118	
Daisy Hill*	502.339.9300	Louisville, KY	
Dransfield & Ross	212.741.7278	54 West 21st Street New York, NY 10010	napkins, placemats, pillows
Fabrica LLC	212.587.6340	New York, NY www.fabricastudio.com	custom work
Feathers	800.382.9967	Pittsburgh, PA	linens; registry
Françoise Nunnalle	212.246.4281	New York, NY	antique linens; by appointment
Frette	310.273.8540	449 North Rodeo Drive Beverly Hills, CA 90210	fine linens
Judi Boisson American Home Collection	631.283.5466	134 Mariner Drive Southampton, NY 11968 www.judiboisson.com	
Just Linens*	212.688.8808 516.283.8808	770 Lexington Ave. New York, NY 10021	tableware and fine linens for special events
Lady of the Cloths	818.986.2843	Sherman Oaks, CA	tablecloths to rent
Kate Morrison	412.731.5196	Pittsburgh, PA Katimo@concentric.net	custom table linens
Kimberly Soles	718.369.9607	179 Seventh Ave. Brooklyn, NY 11215	hand-painted linens, men's accessories

Lillien's Hankicards	360.678.77701	Coupeville, WA	embroidered handkerchiefs
The Linen Gallery	214.522.6700	7001 Preston Rd. Dallas, TX 75205	
Mark Rossi	212.924.0522	668 Greenwich St. New York, NY 10014	custom linens
Meg Cohen Design	212.473.4002	New York, NY	silk and wool table scarves
Monograms by Emily	212.924.4486	New York, NY	machine sewn monograms
The Monogram Shop	631.329.3379	7 Newtown Lane East Hampton, NY 11937	custom embroidery, linens
MU/H Inc.*	212.228.7779	121 E. 24th St. New York, NY 10010 www.mu-h.com	fine table linens and home accessories
Peacock Alley	214.520.6736	3210 Armstrong Ave. Dallas, TX 75205	
Pea Ridge Purties	931.393.2112	323 Marks Avenue Tullahoma, TN 37388	quilts
Pintura Studio*	888.995.8655	New York, NY www.homeportfolio.com	stencilled linens
Richard Fischer	619.232.8808 212.995.8655	San Diego, CA	
Room with a View	310.453.7009	1600 Montana Ave. Santa Monica, CA 90403	
Ruth Fischl	212.273.9710	141 West 28th St. New York, NY 10001	linens to rent
Shaxted by Salvations	310.273.4320	350 N. Camden Dr. Beverly Hills, CA 90210	
Slips	415.362.5652	San Francisco, CA	custom fabrications, slipcovers

R   E   S   O

Susan Parrish	212.645.5020	390 Bleecker St. New York, NY 10014	antique quilts, Americana
Todd Moore Home*	212.989.9088	New York, NY	custom table linens
Trouvaille Française*	212.737.6015	552 East 87th Street New York, NY 10128	antique linens

LOCATIONS

NAME	PHONE	ADDRESS	COMMENTS
Adamson House Museum	310.457.8185	23200 Pacific Coast Hwy. Malibu, CA 90265	
The America Society	212.249.8950	680 Park Ave. New York, NY 10021	landmark residence
The American Club at Kohler	920.451.2107	Highland Dr. Kohler, WI 53044	
Andrea Raisfeld	914.234.9612	Bedford, NY	location scout
Angel Island State Park	415.435.5390	PO Box 318 Tiburon, CA 94920	
Archbishop's Mansion	415.563.7872	1000 Fulton St San Francisco, CA 94117	historic hotel; wedding planning services
Arizona Biltmore	602.954.2540	24th St. & Missouri Ave. Phoenix, AZ 85016	landmark hotel
Atlanta Botanical Gardens	404.876.5859	PO Box 77246 Atlanta, GA 30357	
Auldridge Mead	610.847.5842	Ottsville, PA www.wsmg.com/aulmead	
Avon Old Farms School	860.673.3201	500 Old Farms Rd. Avon, CT 06001 www.avonoldfarms.com	Tudor-style campus

Balclutha	415.929.0202	San Francisco Maritime National Historic Park Hyde St. Pier San Francisco, CA 94133	historic sailing ship
Barley Sheaf Farm	215.794.5104	Holicong, PA www.barleysheaf.com	
Bandelier National Monument	505.672.3861	Los Alamos, NM	
Beck Chapel	812.855.7425	Indiana University Bloomington, IN 47405	
The Beverly Hills Hotel	310.276.2251	9641 Sunset Blvd. Beverly Hills, CA 90210	ballrooms and bungalows
Biltmore Estate	800.408.4405	1 N. Pack Square Asheville, SC 28801	historic mansion
The Biltmore Hotel	305.445.1926	1200 Anastasia Ave. Coral Gables, FL 33134	
The Bishop's Lodge	505.983.6377	PO Box 2367 Santa Fe, NM 87504	mountain chapel and inn
The Blantyre	413.637.3556	Blantyre Rd. Lenox, MA 01240	country estate
Boettcher Mansion on Lookout Mountain	303.526.0855	900 Colorow Rd. Golden, CO 80401	historic mansion
Bonaventura Balloon Co.	800.FLY.NAPA	133 Wall Rd. Napa, CA 94558	
The Boucvalt House	504.528.9771	1025 St. Louis St. New Orleans, LA 70118	historic French Quarter home
Brandywine Mansion/ DuPont Country Club	302.421.1712 302.654.4435	Rockland Road Wilmington, DE 19803	
The Brandywine River Museum	610.388.2700	Chadds Ford, PA	
The Breakers	561.655.6611	1 S. County Rd. Palm Beach, FL 33480	ballrooms and suites

R   E   S   O

Boylan Studios	212.924.7550	601 West 26th Street New York, NY 10001	photo studios for rent, skyline views
Camberly Brown Hotel	502.583.1234	335 W. Broadway Louisville, KY 40202	
Campbell Apartment	212.953.0409	New York, NY	Edwardian apartment, library lounge
The Captain Whidbey Inn	360.678.4097	2072 W. Captain Whidbey Inn Rd. Coupeville, WA 98239	coastline inn
Caramoor	914.232.5035	Katonah, NY	Mediterranean estate
The Carltun	516.542.0700	East Meadon, NY	reception estate
Carnegie Museums of Pittsburgh	412.622.3360	4400 Forbes Ave. Pittsburgh, PA 15213	
Castle Hill Inn & Resort	401.849.3800	590 Ocean Ave. Newport, RI 02840	waterfront inn
Central Park Conservancy*	212.360.2766	New York, NY	formal gardens, terraces
Century Inn	412.945.6600	Scenery Hill, PA 15360	historic inn and formal gardens
Charles Town Landing	803.852.4200	1500 Old Towne Rd. Charleston, SC 29407	
The Charlotte Inn	508.627.4151	27 S. Summer St. Edgartown, MA 02539	
Chateau Marmont	213.656.1010 800.242.8328	8221 Sunset Blvd. Hollywood, CA 90046	
Cheekwood Botanical Gardens	615.353.2148	1200 Forrest Park Dr. Nashville, TN 37205	
Chicago Cultural Center	312.744.6630	78 E. Washington St. Chicago, IL 60602	
Cincinnatian Hotel	513.381.3000	601 Vine St. Cincinnati, OH 45202	landmark hotel

Cindy Lang for Martinsville	207.372.8906	Tenants Harbor, ME www.midcoast.com/ martinsville	Maine farmhouse
Cipriani 42nd Street	212.883.5644	New York, NY	
City Club	415.362.2480	155 Sansome St., Ste 950 San Francisco, CA 94104	historic club
Claussen's Inn	803.765.0440 800.622.3382	2003 Greene St. Columbia, SC 29205	
The Cleveland Ritz-Carlton	216.623.1300	1515 W. Third St. Cleveland, OH 44113	
Cleveland Metro Park Zoo	216.661.6500	3900 Wildlife Way Cleveland, OH 44109	scenic rain forest
The Cloisters of Spanish Monestary	305.945.1462	16711 W. Dixie Hwy. N. Miami Beach, FL 33160	12th-century Gothic monastery
The Colonial Williamsburg Foundation	800.447.8679 757.229.1000	Williamsburg, VA www.history.org	
Colonial Yard	610.666.0485	Audobon, PA	1740's barn near Valley Forge
Dallas Arboretum & Botanical Garden	214.327.8263	8617 Garland Rd. Dallas, TX 75218	
Deer Valley Resort	435.649.1000	PO Box 889 Park City, UT 84060	mountain location
The Delano Hotel	800.555.5001	1685 Collins Ave. Miami Beach, FL 33139	Art Deco hotel
The Delaware River Mills Society	609.397.3586	Stockton, NJ	historic water mill
Denver Design Center	303.733.2455	505 S. Broadway, Ste. 200 Denver, CO 80209	
Disney World Fairy Tale Weddings	407.828.3400	PO Box 1000 Lake Buena Vista, FL 32831	full-service planning available
The Dunhill Hotel	800.354.4141 704.332.4141	237 N. Tryon St. Charlotte, NC 28202	historic hotel

R E S O

Dunsmuir House and Gardens	510.562.0328	2960 Peralta Oaks Court Oakland, CA 94605	
East Brother Light Station	510.233.2385	117 Park Place Pt. Richmond, CA 94801	lighthouse station on a private island
Edgewood Terrace Restaurant	702.588.2787	PO Box 5400 Stateline, NV 89449	
Elizabeth Park	860.722.6541	150 Wallbridge Rd. Hartford, CT 06119	historic municipal park, walled garden
Epping Forest Yacht Club	904.739.7200	1830 Epping Forest Dr. Jacksonville, FL 32217	Mediterranean mansion
Evermay On-The-Delaware	877.864.2365 610.294.9100	River Road Erwinna, PA 18920	historic inn
The Fairmont Hotel	415.772.5293	950 Mason St. San Francisco, CA 94109	
The Fearrington House	919.542.2121	2000 Fearrington Village Center Pittsboro, NC 27312	historic home
Five Star Charters	415.332.0306	85 Liberty Ship Way Sausalito, CA 94965	private charters
The Fogg Museum at Harvard	617.495.0350	32 Quincy St. Cambridge, MA 02138	
Fonthill	215.348.9461	Doylestown, PA	Mediterranean estate, tile works
The Four Seasons Hotel	310.273.2222	300 South Doheny Drive Los Angeles, CA	
Forty Second Street Studios	212.382.4000	229 West 42nd St. New York, NY	glass-walled dance studios
The Fox Theatre	314.534.1111	527 N. Grand Blvd. St. Louis, MO 63103	
The Fulton Lane Inn	843.720.2600	202 King St. Charleston, SC 29401	
The Gamble Mansion	617.267.4430 ext. 707	5 Commonwealth Ave. Boston, MA 02116	historic home

Gardencourt	502.895.3411	c/o Louisville Seminary 1044 Alta Vista Rd. Louisville, KY 40205	19th-century estate
The Georgian Suite	212.734.1468	960 Fifth Ave. New York, NY 10021	
The Georgian Terrace	404.897.1991	659 Peachtree Rd. Atlanta, GA 30308	ballroom
Gibraltor	302.651.9617	Wilmington, DE	historic estate
Grand Romance Riverboat	800.750.7501 707.399.9444	718 Main St., No. 103 Suisun City, CA 94585	
Grant-Humphreys Mansion	303.894.2506	770 Pennsylvania St. Denver, CO 80203	historic home, mountain views
Greystone Mansion	310.550.4654	905 Loma Vista Dr. Beverly Hills, CA 90210	
Haas-Lilienthal House	415.441.5251	San Francisco, CA	Victorian home
Halcyon House	202.338.3295	3400 Prospect St. NW Washington, DC 20007	Georgetown mansion
Halekulani	808.923.2311	2199 Kalia Rd. Honolulu, HI 96815	beachfront views
Hall of State	214.421.4500	3939 Grand Ave. in Fair Park Dallas, TX 75210	
Hamlin Mansion	415.331.0544	2120 Broadway San Francisco, CA 94115	
Harbor View Hotel	508.627.4333	131 N. Water St. Edgartown, MA 02539	gardens, gazebo
Harrison House	516.671.6400	Glen Cove, NY	
Hawaiian Chieftain	415.331.3214	Marine Plaza Sausalito, CA	18th-century square-rig sailboat
The Heathman	503.241.4100	1001 SW Broadway Portland, OR 97205	historic hotel

R   E   S   O

Heritage House	707.937.5885	5200 N. Hwy. 1 Little River, CA 95456	coastal farmhouse inn
Hildene	802.362.1788	Manchester Center, VT	Lincoln homestead
Hornblower Yachts	310.301.6000	13755 Fiji Way Marina del Rey, CA 90292	
Hotel Adolphus	214.742.8200	1321 Commerce St. Dallas, TX 75202	grand hotel
Hotel Bel-Air	310.472.1211	701 Stone Canyon Rd. Los Angeles, CA 90077	garden & pavilion room
Hotel Boulderado	303.442.4344	2115 13th St. Boulder, CO 80302	landmark hotel
Hotel del Coronado	619.435.6611	1500 Orange Ave. Coronado, CA 92118	ballroom
The Hotel du Pont	302.594.3122	11th & Market St. Wilmington, DE 19801	ballroom and suites
Hotel Maison de Ville	800.634.1600	727 Rue Toulouse New Orleans, LA 70130	French Quarter location
Hotel St. Germain	214.871.2516	2516 Maple Ave. Dallas, TX 75201	old world inn
Hyatt Regency Scottsdale at Gainey Ranch	602.991.3388	7500 E. Doubletree Ranch Rd. Scottsdale, AZ 85258	ballroom
Il Cielo	310.276.9990	9018 Burton Way Beverly Hills, CA 90211	garden patio
Indiana Roof Ballroom	317.236.1874	140 W. Washington St. Indianapolis, IN 46204	
Indianapolis Museum of Art	317.923.1331	1200 W. 38th St. Indianapolis, IN 46208	formal garden, river views
Inn at Cedar Falls	740.385.7489	21190 State Route 374 Logan, OH 43138	log cabins and gardens
The Inn at Harvard	617.491.2222	1201 Massachusetts Ave. Cambridge, MA 02138	atrium

The Inn at Little Washington	540.675.3800	Middle and Main Sts. Washington, VA 22747	small inn & dining room
The Inn at Mystic	860.536.9604 800.237.2415	Mystic, CT www.innatmystic.com	
The Inn at Perry Cabin	410.745.2200	308 Watkins Lane St. Michaels, MD 21663	bayfront inn and gardens
Inn at Round Barn Farm	802.496.2266	Waistfield, VT www.innattheroundbarn.com	
Inn at Shelburne Farms	802.985.8498	Shelburne, VT	on Lake Champlain
The Inn at Weathersfield	802.263.9217	Route 106 Weathersfield, VT 05151	Colonial inn
Inn of the Anasazi	505.988.3030	113 Washington Ave. Santa Fe, NM 87501	Adobe-style inn
James Burden Mansion	212.722.4745	7 E. 91st St. New York, NY 10128	historic home
Jody Lexou Yacht Charters	800.662.2628	26 Coddington Wharf Newport, RI 02840	yachts to charter
Judie Robbins	212.633.6440	New York, NY	location scout
James Leary Flood Mansion*	415.563.2900	2222 Broadway San Francisco, CA 94115	historic home with bay views
The John Rutledge House Inn	843.723.7999	116 Broad St. Charleston, SC 29401	historic home with a ballroom
Kenwood Inn & Spa	800.3.KENWOOD 707.833.1293	Kenwood, CA www.kenwoodinn.com	Tuscan setting; cottages
King's Courtyard Inn	843.723.7000	198 King St. Charleston, SC 29401	courtyards
Kualoa Ranch	808.237.8515	PO Box 650 Kaaawa, HI 96730	tropical gardens
Lake Forest Academy	847.234.3210	1500 W. Kennedy Rd. Lake Forest, IL 60045	historic estate

The Landmark Center	651.292.3225	75 W. Fifth St. St. Paul, MN 55102	
The Lark Creek Inn	415.924.7766	234 Magnolia Ave. Larkspur, CA 94939	Victorian house
Le Meridian of Boston	617.451.1900	250 Franklin St. Boston, MA 02110	ballroom
The Legion of Honor	415.221.2233	100 34th Ave. San Francisco, CA 94121	elegant museum café and sculpture garden
Lincoln Park Zoo	312.337.3337	2001 N. Clark St. Chicago, IL 60614	historic city zoo
Little Black Book List	212.334.3364	New York, NY www.littleblackbooklist.com	multi-city location listing
Little Palm Island	305.872.2524	Little Torch Key, FL	south sea style cottages
Locust Grove	502.897.9845	561 Blankenbaker Lane Louisville, KY 40207	18th-century estate and formal gardens
The Lodge & Club at Ponte Vedra Beach	904.273.9500	607 Ponte Vedra Blvd. Ponte Vedra Beach, FL 32082	beach ceremonies and receptions
Longview Mansion	816.761.6669	3361 SW Longview Rd. Lee's Summit, MO 64081	historic landmark
Lyford House	415.388.2524	376 Greenwood Beach Rd. Tiburon, CA 94920	
The Lyman Estate	781.893.7232	185 Lyman St. Waltham, MA 02452	historic mansion and gardens
Magnolia Plantation Hotel	228.832.8400	16391 Robinson Rd. Gulfport, MS 39503	riverside mansion and gardens
Malmaison	314.458.0131	St. Albans Rd., Box 107 St. Albans, MO 63073	French country restaurant
Mandarin Oriental	305.373.0141	601. Brickell Key Dr. Miami, FL www.mandarinoriental.com	grand ballroom

Manhattan Penthouse	212.627.8838	80 Fifth Ave. New York, NY 10011	midtown views
Mansury Mansion	516.878.8862	Center Moriches, NY	historic ballroom
Meadowood Napa Valley Resort	707.963.3646 800.458.8080	900 Meadowood Lane St. Helena, CA 94574	
Memorial Hall	215.334.3472	N. Concourse Dr. off Bellmont Ave. Philadephia, PA 19131	ballroom
Meridian International Center	202.667.6670	1624 Crescent Place NW Washington, DC 20009	historic mansion, formal gardens
Milwaukee Grain Exchange	414.272.6230	Mackie Building 225 E. Michigan St., Ste. 110 Milwaukee, WI 53202	restored landmark
The Mint Museum	704.337.2000	2730 Randolph Rd. Charlotte, NC 28207	
Mission Basilica San Diego del Alcala*	619.281.8449	10818 San Diego Mission Rd. San Diego, CA 92108	original mission gardens
Mission Inn	909.784.0300	3649 Mission Inn Ave. Riverside, CA 92501	gazebo, courtyard, chapel
Missouri Botanical Garden	314.577.5100	4344 Shaw Blvd. St. Louis, MO 63110	
Mohonk Mountain House	800.772.6646 914.255.1000	Lake Mohonk New Paltz, NY www.mohonk.com	Victorian hotel on lake
Mondrian	800.525.8029 323.650.8999	8440 Sunset Blvd. Los Angeles, CA 90069	
Moorings	305.664.4708	Islamorada, FL	beachfront cabins
Morton H. Meyerson Symphony Center	214.670.3600	2301 Flora St. Dallas, TX 75201	
Murat Theatre	317.231.0000	502 N. New Jersey St. Indianapolis, IN 46204	
Myriad Botanical Gardens	405.297.3995	Oklahoma City, OK	

R E S O

Napa Valley Wine Train	707.253.2111 800.427.4124	1275 McKinstry St. Napa, CA 94559	
National Building Museum	202.272.2448	401 F St. NW Washington, DC 20001	
The National Cowboy Hall of Fame and Western Heritage Association	405.478.2250	1700 NE 63rd St. Oklahoma City, OK 73111	
The New York Palace	212.303.7766	455 Madison Ave. New York, NY 10022 www.newyorkpalace.com	ballrooms
Noerenberg Gardens	612.559.6700	2840 N. Shore Dr. Wayzata, MN 55391	lakefront gardens, boathouse
Oak Alley Plantation	504.265.2151	3645 Hwy. 18 Vacherie, LA 70090	historic mansion
Oheka Castle	516.692.2707	Cold Spring Hills, NY www.oheka_castle.com	chateau
Old City Park	214.421.5141	1717 Gano St. Dallas, TX 75215	historic village museum and chapel
Old Federal Reserve Bank Building	415.772.0589	301 Battery St. San Francisco, CA 94111	
The Old Northside Bed & Breakfast	317.635.9123	1340 N. Alabama St. Indianapolis, IN 46202	Victorian mansion with gardens
Opryland Hotel	615.889.1000	2800 Opryland Dr. Nashville, TN 37214	indoor gardens
Otto Kahn Mansion	212.722.4747	1 E. 91st St. New York, NY 10028	historic residence
The Park Hyatt	800.221.0833 215.893.1776	1415 Chancellor Court Philadephia, PA 19102	
The Pavilion of the Two Sisters	504.488.2896	1 Palm Dr. New Orleans, LA 70124	formal gardens

The Peabody Hotel	901.529.4000	149 Union Ave. Memphis, TN 38103	
Peach Grove Inn	914.986.7411 800.237.2415	Warwick, NY www.peachgroveinn.com	19th-century farmhouse inn
Pelligrini Vineyards	631.734.4111	Cutchogue, NY www.pelligrinivineyard.com	vineyard with central tentable courtyard
Pennsbury Inn	610.388.1435	Chadds Ford, PA	
The Pfister Hotel	414.273.8222	424 E. Wisconsin Ave. Milwaukee, WI 53202	landmark hotel
Philipsburg Manor	914.631.8200	Route 9 Sleepy Hollow, NY 10591	working colonial farm
Phipps Conservatory	412.622.6915	1 Schenley Park Pittsburgh, PA 15213	indoor gardens
Phipps Mansion	303.777.4441	3400 Belcaro Dr. Denver, CO 80209	Georgian mansion
Phipps Tennis Pavilion	303.777.4441	3300 Belcaro Dr. Denver, CO 80209	
The Phoenician	602.941.8200	6000 E. Camelback Rd. Scottsdale, AZ 85251	cactus garden
The Pierre	212.838.8000	2 E. 61st St. New York, NY 10021	
Pittsburgh Center for the Arts	412.361.0873	6300 Fifth Ave. Pittsburgh, PA 15232	
Pittsburgh's Grand Hall at the Priory	412.231.3338	614 Pressley St. Pittsburgh, PA 15212	European-style inn
Places	212.737.7536	Box 810 Gracie Sta. New York, NY 10028	location directory
The Plaza Hotel	800.527.4727	New York, NY www.fairmont.com	full-service hotel and ballrooms
The Point	800.255.3530 518.891.5674	HCR #1 Box 65 Saranac Lake, NY 12983	rustic luxury lake front inn

The Polo Fields Country Club	734.998.1555	5200 Polo Fields Dr. Ann Arbor, MI 48103	ballroom
Potomac Boat Club	202.333.9737	3530 Water St. NW Washington, DC 20007	
Powell Gardens	816.697.2600	1609 NW U.S. Highway 50 Kingsville, MO 64061	botanical gardens and landmark chapel
Powell Symphony Hall	314.533.2500 314.286.4148	718 N. Grand Blvd. St. Louis, MO 63103	
The Pratt Mansions	212.744.4486	1027 Fifth Ave. New York, NY 10028	historic residence
Prospect Hill	800.277.0844	2887 Poindexter Rd. Trevilians, VA 23093	historic plantation
The Puck Building	212.274.8900	New York, NY	landmark building ballrooms
Rainbow Room	212.632.5000	30 Rockefeller Plaza New York, NY 10112	stellar views
El Rancho De Las Golondrinas	505.471.2261	334 Los Pinos Rd. Santa Fe, NM 87505	historic village
The Randall Davey Audubon Center	505.983.4609	PO Box 9314 Santa Fe, NM 87504	historic estate
Red Butte Garden and Arboretum	801.585.5225	300 Wakara Way Salt Lake City, UT 84108	
Rembrandt's Restaurant	816.436.8700	2820 NW Barry Rd. Kansas City, MO 64154	rose garden
Rex Hill Vineyard	503.538.0666	30835 N. Hwy. 99W Newberg, OR 97132	
Rittenhouse Hotel	215.546.9000	210 W. Rittenhouse Square Philadelphia, PA 19103	
The Ritz-Carlton St. Louis	314.863.6300	100 Carondelet Plaza St. Louis, MO 63105	
The Ritz-Carlton Philadelphia	215.563.1600	17th and Chestnut St. at Liberty Place Philadelphia, PA 19103	

River Oaks Garden Club	713.523.2483	2503 Westheimer Rd. Houston, TX 77098	banquet hall and formal gardens
The Riverplace Hotel	503.228.3233	1510 SW Harbor Way Portland, OR 97201	
Royal Hawaiian Hotel	808.923.7311	2259 Kalakaua Ave. Honolulu, HI 96815	beachfront views
Rock and Roll Hall of Fame	216.781.7625	1 Key Plaza Cleveland, OH 44114	
The Ruins	206.285.7846	570 Roy St. Seattle, WA 98109	interior garden
St. Albans Studio	314.458.5356	St. Albans, MO	stone residence
The Saint Louis Art Museum	314.721.0072	1 Fine Arts Dr. St. Louis, MO 63110	
St. Louis Zoo	314.768.5411	Forest Park St. Louis, MO 63110	lakeside café
St. Michaels Crab House	410.745.3737	St. Michaels, MD	docks, marina
St. Paulus Church and Social Hall	415.763.8088	930 Gough St. San Francisco, CA 94102	
Saddle Peak Lodge	818.222.3888	419 Gold Canyon Rd. Calabasas, CA 91302	
Saddlerock Ranch	818.889.0008	31727 Mulholland Hwy. Malibu, CA 90265	working ranch
Saguaro Lake Ranch Resort	602.984.2194	13020 Bush Hwy. Mesa, AZ 85215	
San Ysidro Ranch	805.969.5046	900 San Ysidro Lane Montecito, CA 93108	barn, bungalows, and formal garden
Schnull Rauch House	317.925.4600	3050 N. Meridian St. Indianapolis, IN 46208	
Seelbach Hotel	502.585.3200	500 Fourth Ave. Louisville, KY 40202	

R E S O

Seven Gables Inn	314.863.8400	26 N. Meramec St. Louis, MO 63105	
Sherry Mills Winery	313.668.4817	Ann Arbor, MI	
Shutters on the Beach	310.458.0030	1 Pico Blvd. Santa Monica, CA 90405	
Sir Francis Drake Hotel	415.392.7755	450 Powell St. San Francisco, CA 94102	
Skansonia Ferryboat	206.545.9109	2505 N. Northlake Way Seattle, WA 98103	dry-docked lakeside ferry
Smash Box Studio	310.558.7660	8549 Hiquera St. Culver City, CA 90232	photography studios for events
Snowbird Ski and Summer Resort	801.742.2222	PO Box 929000 Snowbird, UT 84092	
The Stanhope Hotel	212.288.5800	995 Fifth Ave. New York, NY 10028	
Sterling Vineyards	707.942.3300 707.942.3359	1111 Dunaweal Lane Calistoga, CA 94515	
Stimson Green Mansion	206.624.0474	1204 Minor Ave. Seattle, WA 98101	
Stone Manor	310.457.6285	Malibu, CA	ocean-view estate
Stow Acres Country Club	978.568.8690	58 Randall Rd. Stow, MA 01775	
Stowehof Inn and Resort	800.932.7136	434 Edison Hill Rd. Stowe, VT 05672	Swiss-Austrian style resort
Strathmore Hall	301.530.0540	10701 Rockville Pike N. Bethesda, MD 20852	former estate
Studio 450	212.290.1400	450 W. 31st St. New York, NY 10001	loft with outdoor terraces
Sundance Resort	801.225.4107	R.R. 3, Box A-1 Sundance, UT 84604	

Swedenborgian Church	415.346.6466	2107 Lyon St. San Francisco, CA 94115	Mission-style chapel, walled garden
Tanque Verde Ranch	520.296.6275	14301 E. Speedway Tucson, AZ 85748	
Tega Cay Golf Club	803.548.3500	1 Molokai Dr. Tega Cay, SC 29715	
Temple Emanu-El	415.751.2535	2 Lake St. San Francisco, CA 94118	open-air courtyard
The Tides	800.OUTPOST 305.604.5000	1220 Ocean Drive. Miami Beach, FL 33139 www.islandoutpost.com	
Thistle Hill	817.336.1212	1509 Pennsylvania Ave. Fort Worth, TX 76104	historic home
Thomas Bennett House	843.720.1203	69 Barre St. Charleston, SC 29401	historic home and gardens
Thomas Fogarty Winery and Vineyards	650.851.6777	19501 Skyline Blvd. Woodside, CA 94062	pavilion
Tinicum Park	215.348.6114 x3311	Erwinna, PA	state park with large wood barn for events
Union Station	213.625.5865	800 N. Alameda St. Los Angeles, CA 90012	
Union Station Hotel	615.726.1001	1001 Broadway Nashville, TN 37203	
Victoria House Inn	843.720.2944 800.933.5464	208 King St. Charleston, SC 29401	
Villa Montalvo	408.741.3421	15400 Montalvo Rd. Saratoga, CA 95070	
Villas International	800.221.2260	San Rafael, CA	overseas rentals
Vizcaya Museum & Gardens	305.250.9133	3251 S. Miami Ave. Miami, FL 33129	

R E S O

The Waterford Hotel	800.992.2009 405.848.4782	6300 Waterford Blvd. Oklahoma City, OK 73118	
Wave Hill	718.549.7368	675 W. 252nd St. Bronx, NY 10471	historic estate with river view
Waveny House	203.966.0502	New Caanan, CT	historic estate
The Weisman Art Museum	612.625.9494	333 E. River Rd. University of Minnesota Minneapolis, MN 55455	
Westerfield House	618.539.5643	8059 Jefferson Rd. Freeburg, IL 62243	rustic home and gardens
Westin William Penn Hotel	412.553.5029	Pittsburgh, PA	wedding consultant
Whitehall	502.897.2944	3110 Lexington Rd. Louisville, KY 40206	historic estate
Whitely Creek	877.985.9275	Brainerd, MN	secluded getaway
Willow Ridge Manor	303.697.6951	4903 Willow Springs Rd. Morrison, CO 80465	historic mansion
Willowisp Country Club	281.437.8217	14502 Fondren Rd. Missouri City, TX 77489	
Windsor Court Hotel	504.524.6000	300 Gravier St. New Orleans, LA 70130	
Woodlawn Mansion	301.652.9188 ext. 3021	8940 Jones Mill Rd. Chevy Chase, MD 20815	historic mansion and wildlife conservatory
Woodruff-Fontaine House	901.526.1469	680 Adams Ave. Memphis, TN 38105	historic mansion
The World Forrestry Center	503.228.1367 ext. 101	4033 SW Canyon Rd. Portland, OR 97221	
Wrigley Mansion Club	602.955.4079	2501 E. Telawa Trail Phoenix, AZ 85016	

MUSIC & DANCE

NAME	PHONE	ADDRESS	COMMENTS
A. Weist Entertainment Group	631.754.0594	Fort Salonga, NY www.stanwiest.com	full service music broker
Archive of Contemporary Music	212.226.6967	54 White New York, NY www.archmusic.com	research organization
Baguette Quartet	510.528.3723	San Francisco, CA	
Bud Maltin	201.444.7001 212.447.6543	Ridgewood, NJ www.budmaltin.com	
Curtis Music & Entertainment	908.352.3131	Elizabeth, NJ	string, brass, woodwind ensembles, orchestras and chamber groups
Doug Winters Music	914.769.0103	Pleasantville, NY	dance band and vocalists
Eclypse	302.322.1076	Wilmington, DE	jazz ensemble
El Mariachi	215.567.6060	Philadelphia, PA	traditional mariaches
Festival Brass	214.328.9330	Dallas, TX	brass musicians
Hank Lane Music and Productions	212.767.0600 516.829.4111	New York, NY	orchestras, vocals, rock & standards
Janet King	516.671.4519	Long Island, NY	classical harpist
Jeff Robbins	214.414.2645	Dallas, TX	jazz trios to contemporary quartets
Ladies Choice String Quartet	310.391.3762	Los Angeles, CA	
Lester Lanin Orchestras	212.265.5208	New York, NY	
Los Santos	212.828.2109	New York, NY	Cuban jazz
Majestic Brass	516.472.5363	Holbrook, NY	trumpeters

RESO

Marcom Savoy and the Hurricanes	415.331.3539	San Francisco, CA	
Music In The Air	212.946.1563 800.332.9705	www.musicintheair.com	jazz ensemble
New York City Swing	718.848.9442	New York, NY	
Paul Lindemeyer Trio	914.693.9055	Livingston, NY	classic jazz
Peggy Cone Entertainment	212.734.1361	New York, NY	vocalist, 30's – 40's songs a specialty
Peter Duchin	212.972.2260	New York, NY	orchestra
Planet Tango		planet-tango.com	tango lessons by appointment
Preferred Artists	800.477.8558	Ridgefield, CT	artist representative; swing, R & B a specialty
Richard Connick Group	718.545.9638 718.596.8740	New York, NY	jazz standards
SPN Music	516.767.3919	Port Washington, NY www.spnmusic.com	entertainment and music broker
Sterling Music Ensembles	212.481.7697	New York, NY	chamber music
Sterling Trio Flute, Violin and Cello	510.524.2569	San Francisco, CA	
Swing Fever	415.459.2428	San Francisco, CA	
Tlaquapaque	714.528.8515	Plascenscia, CA	mariache music
Trinidad International Steelband	415.346.4646	San Francisco, CA	
Vali Productions	415.459.2428	San Francisco, CA	

NAME	PHONE	ADDRESS	COMMENTS
The Vicho Vincencio Band	214.644.6846	Dallas, TX	
Vonette Yanaginuma	818.365.4065	Beverly Hills, CA	harpist
Willow Productions	212.571.6931 201.768.9100	New York, NY www.vali.com	

PARTY EQUIPMENT & RENTALS

NAME	PHONE	ADDRESS	COMMENTS
Abbey Party Tents	214.350.5373	Dallas, TX	equipment too
Chuppahs on Hudson	888.CHUPPAH	Croton-on-Hudson, NY	custom wedding canopies
Classic Party Rentals	944.223310.202.0011	Culver City, CA	
Design Within Reach	1.800.944.2233	San Francisco, CA www.dwr.com	café chairs and bistro tables for purchase
Ducky Bob's Cannonball Party Rentals	972.381.8000	Carrollton, TX	tents too
Durkin Awning	800.498.3028 203.748.2142	Danbury, CT	tents, awnings, flagpoles
Fox Tent & Awning	734.665.9126	617 South Ashley St. Ann Arbor, MI 48104	
Frost Lighting	708.729.8200	Northbrook, IL	full-service lighting, special effects
Hudson Valley Tent Co.	800.255.2698	Montgomery, NY	
J.G. Willis	617.527.0037	Boston, MA	tent rentals

RESO

OK Uniform Company	212.791.9789	New York, NY www.okuniform.com	uniforms and white cotton aprons
Party Rental	201.517.8750 888.774.4776	Teterboro, NJ	
Partytime Rentals	317.844.5178	1212 S. Range Line Rd. Carmel, IN 46032	
Partytime Tents & Rentals	973.948.2426	Branchville, NJ	
Peterson Party Center	781.729.4000	Boston, MA	rentals
Premier Party Servers	800.PARTY.HELP	New York, NY	staff for parties
The Prop Company	212.691.7767	New York, NY	vintage, contemporary accessories to rent
Props for Today	212.244.9600	New York, NY www.propsfortoday.com	vintage and contemporary decorative accessories for rent
Resource One	818.343.3451	6925 Canby Ave. Reseda, CA 91335	
Ruth Fischl*	212.273.9710	141 West 28th St. New York, NY 10001 www.ruthfischl.com	linens, decorative accessories for rent
Service Party Rental*	212.752.7661 718.381.6000	770 Lexington Avenue New York, NY 10021	full-service rentals; primary providors of equipment for this book
Something Different	212.772.0516	Paterson, NJ	tabletop & chairs
Starr Tents	800.466.4811 914.667.2001	Mount Vernon, NY	rentals
Stortz Lighting	800.837.8617 212.219.2330	70 Laight St. New York, NY 10021	full-service lighting, special effects
Taylor Rental	631.298.4323	Main Rd. Mattituck, NY 11952	rentals for parties

Unique Event Resources	818.343.3451	Reseda, CA	table linens for rent
Umbrellatime.com	800.823.6677	Sarasota, FL www.umbrellatime.com	thatched and canvas market umbrellas
Watts Up!	323.465.2000	Hollywood, CA	

PHOTOGRAPHY & VIDEOGRAPHY

NAME	PHONE	ADDRESS	COMMENTS
Aimee Rentmeester	323.878.0044	Los Angeles, CA	
Alex Berliner	213.857.1282	23 N. La Brea Ave. Los Angeles, CA 90036	
Amber Productions	805.964.4533	Santa Barbara, CA	video documentation
Anthony Israel	718.387.4886 917.405.5125	Brooklyn, NY	photojournalistic style
Babboni's Creative Imaging	414.328.3211	8306 W. Lincoln Ave. West Allis, WI 53219	
Bachrach Photographs	617.536.4730	647 Boylston St. Boston, MA 02116	formal portraits
Bachrach Studio	800.277.9077 212.755.6233	New York, NY	formal portraits
Beth Herzhaft	323.653.2364	Los Angeles, CA	
Beverly Hall Photography	508.228.2147	Nantucket, MA	also black and white
B & H	800.606.6969 212.444.6615	New York, NY www.bhphotovideo.com	professional photography supplies
Bresner Studios	215.546.7277	6729 Castor Ave. Philadelphia, PA 19149	

RESO

Cary Hazlegrove Photography	508.228.3783 512.452.6181	Nantucket, MA Austin, TX	also black and white
Cheryl Klauss	212.431.3569	New York, NY	formal portraits
Cilento	414.964.6161	1409 E. Capital Dr. Milwaukee, WI 53217	
Denis Reggie Photographers	800.379.1999 404.873.8080	Atlanta, GA	available in New York, Los Angeles
Fisher Photography	802.496.5215 541.387.5954	Waitsfield, VT Hood River, OR www.madriver.com/fisher	formal portraits
Frank Lopez Photography	877.321.5411	Dallas, TX	black and white; custom albums
Fred Marcus Photography & Videography	212.873.5588	New York, NY www.fredmarcus.com	formal portraits, videography
Gareth Rockliffe	978.927.6962	Beverly, MA	black and white, hand tinting; custom albums
Geoff Winningham	713.526.6175	Houston, TX www.geoffwinningham.com	
George Long	800.318.4516 504.282.3559	New Orleans, LA	
Grevy Photography	504.866.5093	7433 Maple St. New Orleans, LA 70118	portraits
Gruber Photographers	212.262.9777	New York, NY www.gruberphotographers.com	
Hal Slifer	800.234.7755 617.787.7910	Boston, MA	videography
Harold Hechler Assoc.	212.72.6565	654 Madison Ave. New York, NY 10021	
Heirloom Restoration	203.795.0565	Orange, CT	photographic restoration
Hilary N. Bullock Photography	612.338.7516	529 S. Seventh St., Ste. 555 Minneapolis, MN 55415	

Hi-Tech PhotoImaging	516.931.8631	Plainview, NY	will scan photos to CDs
Holger Thoss	212.627.8829	New York, NY	
Jack Caputo	310.273.6181	493 S. Robertson Blvd. Beverly Hills, CA 90211	
James French Photography	214.368.0990	8411 Preston Ave., Ste. 188 Dallas, TX 75225	by appointment
Jamie Bosworth Photography	503.246.5378	8635 SW Ninth St. Portland, OR 97219	
Jasper-Sky	800.357.8011 201.222.8011	Jersey City, NJ	
Jeannie Frey Rhodes	225.927.8282	Baton Rouge, LA	
Jenny Bissell	440.247.7988	Cleveland, OH	
Jeff Harris Photography	212.334.0125	New York, NY	
John Derryberry & Associates	214.357.5457	5757 W. Lovers Lane, Ste. 310 Dallas, TX 75209	also black and white; by appointment
John Dolan	212.462.2598	New York, NY	also black and white
John Tilley Photography	214.358.4747	Dallas, TX www.johntilley photography.com	also portraits
John Wolfsohn	310.859.9266	9904 Durant Dr. Beverly Hills, CA 90212	
Joyce Wilson	317.786.1769	Indianapolis, IN	also portraits
Julie Skarratt	212.877.2604	New York, NY	also handmade albums
Kaish.Dahl	310.724.7282	9400 Santa Monica Blvd. Beverly Hills, CA 90210	
Joyce Wilson	317.786.1769	Indianapolis, IN	also portraits

R E S O

Karen Hill Photography	212.529.6926	New York, NY	
Keith Trumbo	212.580.7104	New York, NY	
Laurence Lauterborn Photography	415.863.1132	San Francisco, CA	
Laurie Klein	203.740.1110	Brookville, CT ww.laurieklein.com	infrared and hand-tinted portraits a specialty
Lifestyle Photography	408.294.5545	San Jose, CA	
Longshots	504.282.3559	1505 Gardena Dr. New Orleans, LA 70122	
Maureen Edwards De Fries Photography	203.924.2375	Shelton, CT www.maureenedwards defries.com	portraits, custom albums
Maxine Henryson Photography	212.673.2918	New York, NY www.maxinephotography.com	
Mike Posey Photography and Video	504.488.8000	3524 Canal St. New Orleans, LA 70119	also videography
Nancy Cohn Photography	802.253.9641 VT 408.395.9030 CA 407.842.1875 FL	Stowe, VT	
Nelson Hume	212.222.7424	New York, NY	videography and editing services
Philippe Cheng Photography	212.627.4262	New York, NY	
Phil Kramer Photography	215.928.9189	30 S. Bank St. Philadelphia, PA 19106	
Rob Fraser	212.941.0433	New York, NY	also portraits
Robert Friedel	212.477.3452	New York, NY	also black and white
Robert George	314.771.6622	1933 Edwards Ave. St. Louis, MO 63110	also black and white

Robin Sachs Photography	214.824.0624	Dallas, TX	portraits only, also black and white
Ross Whitaker Studio	212.279.2600	New York, NY www.rosswhitaker.com	
Sengbush Photography	214.363.3264	6611 Snyder Plaza, Ste. 109 Dallas, TX 75205	
Sarah Merians Photography Inc.	212.633.0502	New York, NY www.sarahmerians.com	
Scott Whittle Photography	718.522.1242	Brooklyn, NY	
Shadows and Light Photography	510.632.5886	Oakland, CA	
S. M. Cooper Photography	800.814.4794	8549 Hiquera St. Culver City, CA 90232	photography studios
Stephen Photography	502.244.3753 203.878.6825	Bethany, CT www.smcooper.com	
Steven E. Gross & Associates	773.509.9398	Chicago, IL www.reallifeweddings.com	black and white a specialty
Susan Bloch Photography	631.549.0203	Long Island, NY	
Tanya Malott Lawson*	787.721.1232	San Juan, Puerto Rico	also black and white
Terri Bloom Photography	212.475.2274	New York, NY www.teribloom.com/weddings	
Tom Fitzsimmons	970.925.3487	Aspen, CO	
Valerie Shaff	212.965.1080	New York, NY	portraits
Wendi Schneider Photography & Design	303.322.2246	Denver, CO	hand-painted images
W. Gregory Puls	317.293.9920	Indianapolis, IN	

R E S O

NAME	PHONE	ADDRESS	COMMENTS
Willis Preston Campbell	888.425.5700 831.425.5700	Santa Cruz, CA www.wpcphotography.com	
Zalewa Image Designers	800.836.7688 812.951.3259 502.451.0307	9700 State Rd. 64 Georgetown, IN 47122	

PROVISIONS

NAME	PHONE	ADDRESS	COMMENTS
Albert Uster	800.231.8154	Gaitherburg, MD	imported food
American Beer Distributing Company	718.875.0226	Brooklyn, NY	microbrews
Aristoff Caviar and Fine Foods	310.271.0576 718.433.2726 800.332.7478	West Hollywood, CA New York, NY	caviar, pâtés, mustards, oils; mail order
Black Hound	212.979.9505 800.344.4417	149 First Ave. New York, NY 10030	fine cookies, gifts; mail order
Browne Trading Company	207.766.2402 800.332.7478	West Hollywood, CA	fine provisions by mail
Caviarteria	212.759.7410 310.285.9773	New York, NY Beverly Hills, CA www.caviarteria.com	
Ciao Bella	800.435.2863	231 40th Street Irvington, NJ	custom ice creams
CMC Company	800.262.2780	Avalon, NJ	ethnic foodstuffs; mail order
Cones Ice Creams	212.414.1795	New York, NY	
The Cook Inspired	800.693.3342	Rhinebeck, NY	sweet tarts
David Wehrs Seafood	800.262.2780	St. Michaels, MD	Chesapeake Bay crabs a specialty

Dean & DeLuca	212.431.1691 800.221.7714	560 Broadway New York, NY 10012 www.deandeluca.com	mail order available
Dufour Pastry Kitchens	212.929.2800	25 Ninth Avenue New York, NY	handmade frozen puff pastry, hors d'oeuvres, empanadas, tart shells
El Cholo	888.982.6253		tamales
Elia and Jules Esposito's Porchetta	215.271.8418	1627 S. Tenth St. Philadelphia, PA 19148	Italian specialties; some mail order
Feastivities	817.377.3011	5724 Lock Ave. Fort Worth, TX 76107	gourmet foods and fresh caviar
Four Winds Specialties	212.366.5270	58 Gansevoort Street New York, NY	exotic vegetables
Honeybaked Ham	800.892.HAMS	Toledo, OH	mail order, smoked meats
Ice Sculpture Designs	516.243.3360	Deer Park, NY www.icesculpture.com	
Kalustyan's	212.685.3451	123 Lexington Avenue www.kalustysans.com	Oriental, Middle Eastern & Indian foods
The Lobster Place	213.278.9750	Chelsea Market New York, NY www.lobsterplace.com	fresh seafood
Malibu Farms	213.278.9750	S. San Pedro, CA	edible pansies
Mahattan Frutier*	800.841.5718	105 East 29th Street New York, NY www.manhattanfrutier.com	fruit baskets, hampers
Marty's	214.526.4070	3316 Oakland Ave. Dallas, TX 75219	fresh caviar
New York Beverage	212.831.4000	New York, NY	unusual varieties beer a specialty
JP Shellfish Company	207.439.6018	Eliot, ME	lobsters, oysters

R   E   S   O

Petrossian	212.245.2217	New York, NY	caviar, mail order
Ravioli Store	212.925.1737	New York, NY	custom pastas
St. Clair Ice Cream Company	203.853.4774	South Norwalk, CT	floral and novelty shaped sorbets
St. Michaels Seafood	410.745.3737	St. Michaels, MD	
Uglesich's	504.523.8571	New Orleans, LA	bayou specialties
Wild Edibles	212.334.1801	New York, NY	specialty seafood
Zingerman's	888.636.8162	Ann Arbor, MI wwwzingerman's.com	fancy food emporium

RIBBONS

NAME	PHONE	ADDRESS	COMMENTS
Angelsea	209.948.8428	Stockton, CA	
A Touch of Ivy	609.252.1191	Princeton, NJ	cotton ribbons
Bell'occhio	415.864.4048	8 Brady St. San Francisco, CA 94103	antique ribbons
Brimar Inc.*	847.831.2120 800.274.1205	Highland Park, IL	metallic cording, tassels
C.M. Offray & Son, Inc.*	212.279.9776	Chester, NJ www.offray.com	call for local availability
Cinderella Flowers	212.840.0644 212.564.2929	48 West 38th Street New York, NY 10018	trimmings, silk flowers
Cream City Ribbons	414.277.1221	Milwaukee, WI	cotton ribbons
Gardener's Ribbons & Lace	817.640.1436	2235 E. Division Arlington, TX 76011	vintage ribbons

Hanah Silk	888.321.HANA	Arcata, CA	hand-dyed ribbons
Hyman Hendler & Lace	212.840.8393	New York, NY	vintage and import ribbon emporium
Impressions/ Just Accents*	888.389.0550 212.481.6127	New York, NY	wired silk organza ribbons
International Silks & Woolens	213.653.6453	8347 Beverly Blvd. Los Angeles, CA 90048	
Kel-Toy	415.641.4885	San Francisco, CA	craft paper ribbons, raffia
Loose Ends	503.390.7457	Salem, OR www.looseends.com	paper ribbons
Majunga	203.467.0003	New Haven, CT	raffia braided ribbons
Midori	800.659.3049 206.282.3595	Seattle, WA www.midoriribbon.com	organza, silk ribbons
Mokuba	503.390.7457	Salem, OR www.looseends.com	paper ribbons
Moskatel's	212.869.8900 212.302.5010	55 West 39th Street New York, NY 10018	decorative ribbons
Paulette C. Knight	800.642.8900 415.626.6184	San Francisco, CA	wired, silk ribbons; call for local availability
Renaissance Buttons	312.883.9508	826 West Armitage Ave. Chicago, IL 60614	Victorian trimmings, buttons
Renaissance Buttons	415.626.6184	San Francisco, CA	wired, silk ribbons
The Ribbonry	419.872.0073	119 Louisiana Ave. Perrysburg, OH 43551	
Ruban Et Fleur	310.641.3466	8655 Sepulveda Blvd. Los Angeles, CA 90045	imported ribbons
Sweet Material Things	914.894.2519	Walkill, NY	ribbonwork accessories

R E S O

Tender Buttons	212.758.7004 312.337.7033	New York, NY Chicago, IL	vintage buttons
V V Rouleaux	011.01.71.730.3125	55 Sloane Sq. London, England	ribbon, trimmings, braids; mail order
Vaban	800.448.9988	Brisbane, CA	imported silk, wired ribbons

STATIONERY

NAME	PHONE	ADDRESS	COMMENTS
Aesthete	401.846.6324	Newport, RI	invitations
Alexander Wood Studios	800.721.59357	Barrington, IL www.alexanderwood.com	hand-illustrated notecards
Alpine Creative Group	800.289.6507 212.989.4198	159 West 25th Street New York, NY 10001	full-service invitation studio
Arak Kanofsky Studios*	610.330.9423	1110 Northhamton St. Easton, PA 18042	custom invitations, printmaking studio
B. Designs	978.374.3575	Haverhill, MA	letterpress design
Barbara Logan's Paperworks	301.774.2949	Rockville, MD	
Barbara Margolis	212.988.6256	New York, NY	design
The Beverley Collection	904.387.2625	4217 Chippewa Drive Jacksonville, FL 32210	engraved invitations
Blue Marmalade	877.597.2023 612.788.8517	Minneapolis, MN	computer-generated invitations
Bowne & Co.	212.748.8652 212.669.9400	211 Water Street New York, NY 10038	letterpress

BOHO Designs	415.441.1617	San Francisco, CA	custom invitations
Bumblebee Press	800.764.9740 404.577.4540	Atlanta, GA www.bumblebeepress.com	notecards with pressed flowers, invitations
Campbell Stationers & Engravers	214.692.8380	Dallas, TX	
Cartier	212.753.0111	New York, NY	engraved stationery
Century Marketing	419.354.2591 800.537.9429	Bowling Green, OH	custom labels
Claudia Laub Studio	323.931.1710	7404 Beverly Blvd. Los Angeles, CA 90036	letterpress
Cottage Industries	203.266.9075	Westport, CT	graphic design
Couturier de Cardboard	212.243.2225	New York, NY	custom invitations, stationery items
Crane & Co. Papermakers	617.247.2822	Prudential Center 800 Boylston St. Boston, MA 02199	calligraphy available
Crane & Company*	800.IS.CRANE 413.684.2600	Dalton, MA www.crane.com	fine papers and "Blue Book," a guide of stationery ettiquette
Creative Intelligence	323.936.9009	4988 Venice Blvd. Los Angeles, CA 90019	custom invitations
Custom Tape & Label Company	800.525.1075 602.908.2525	Denver, CO	prints custom labels
Dempsey & Carroll	212.486.7526 202.331.0550	New York, NY Washington, DC	
Elements	949.854.3690	Irvine, CA	custom card bar
Ellen Weldon Designs*	212.925.4483	273 Church St. New York, NY 10013	custom invitations, calligraphy
Embrey Papers	310.440.2620	11965 San Vincente Blvd. Los Angeles, CA 90049	

R E S O

Empire Stamp & Seal	212.679.5370	New York, NY	embossers, custom rubber stamps
English Card Co.	516.520.6632	Sayville, NY	collage details
Enid Wilson	718.384.8814	Brooklyn, NY	custom invitations
Envelopments	714.258.2900 800.335.3536	Tustin, CA	custom wedding invitations
Fox River Paper Company		Appleton, WI	custom watermarks
Francis-Orr	310.271.6106	Beverly Hills, CA	
The French Corner	800.421.4367 914.945.8414	Elmsford, NY www.frenchcorner.com	inks, wax seals
Hannah	847.864.8292	Evanston, IL	handmade cards
Hollis Hills Mill*	718.217.4846	Hollis Hills, NY	handmade paper maker, custom invitations
Hudon Street Papers	212.229.1064	357 Bleecker Street New York, NY	
I.H.M. Systems	516.589.5600	Bohemia, NY	full-service printer
Index Print Media	212.979.6878	New York, NY www.indexpm.com	embossed stationery
J & M Martinez Graphique de France	800.444.1464	9 State St. Woburn, MA 01801	letterpress stationery, journals; call for local availability
✓ **Jam Paper**	212.255.4593	611 Ave. of the Americas New York, NY 10011 www.jampaper.com	paper stock
Joy Designs	888.JOYDESIGN	Westport, CT	earth-friendly papers
Judith Winslow Printers	510.654.6416	Emeryville, CA www.julieholcomb	stationery, paper, product design
Julie Holcomb Printers	516.589.5600	Bohemia, NY printers.com	full-service printer
Just Robin	310.273.9736	9171 Wilshire Blvd. Beverly Hills, CA 90210	

Kate's Paperie*	212.941.9816	561 Broadway New York, NY 10012	custom invitations, ribbons, albums, gifts
	212.396.3670	1282 Third Ave. New York, NY 10021	
	212.633.0570	8 W. 13th St. New York, NY 10011 www.katespaperie.com	
Katushka	206.632.3227	Seattle, WA www.katushka.com	decorative adhesive seals
La Papeterie St-Armand*	514.931.8338	Montreal, Quebec	handmade paper circles for cake tables
Menash Signatures	800.pen.shop	New York, NY	fine writing instruments
Mira Aster Novelties	718.486.3275	Brooklyn, NY	hinged place cards
Modern Postcard	619.431.7084 800.959.8365	Carlsbad, CA	custom postcards from any artwork
100th Monkey Productions	818.398.3132	Pasadena, CA	pre-printed stationery, Polaroid transfer images
Mrs. John L. Strong	212.838.3848	699 Madison Ave. New York, NY 10021	custom engraving
Nancy Sharon Collins Stationer	212.431.5959	New York, NY	hand-engraved stationery
Old Print Factory	800.325.5383	New Baltimore, MI	antique print reproductions, papers
Orange Art	800.253.8975	Woodstock, CT	contemporary place cards
Ordning & Reda	212.421.8199	1305 3rd Avenue New York, NY 10021	contemporary Swedish paper goods
Paper Access	800.PAPER.01 973.992.1300	New York, NY Livingston, NJ www.paperaccess.com	papers, embossing supplies; catalog
The Paper Garden	210.494.9602	San Antonio, TX	stationery, rubber stamps
Paper Place	512.451.6531	4001 N. Lamar Blvd. Austin, TX 78756	stationery, fine papers

Paper Routes	214.828.9494	Dallas, TX	handmade papers
Papers	801.530.0293	Salt Lake City, UT	
Papivore	212.627.6055	117 Perry Street New York, NY	fine papers and albums
Papyrus	800.355.8099 212.717.0002	852 Lexington Ave. New York, NY 10021 www.bestselections. com/papyrus	
Pendragon, Ink*	508.234.6843	27 Prospect St. Whitinsville, MA 01581	custom invitations, calligraphy, programs, scrolls, place cards
Peter Koch, Printer	510.849.0673	Berkeley, CA	handmade papers
Phillip Howlett & Jeff Botwin	415.441.1617	San Francisco, CA	graphic designers
Pineapple Design	718.965.3228	Brooklyn, NY	custom invitations
Printemps	203.226.6869	Westport, CT	custom stationers
The Printery	516.922.3250	43 W. Main St. Oyster Bay, NY 11771	letterpress stationery
Prometheus	949.240.1052	Capistrano Beach, CA www.prometheusgifts.com	glass pens, Italian inks, albums
Prose and Letters	408.293.1852	San Jose, CA	custom stationery
PS The Letter	817.731.2032	5122 Camp Bowie Blvd. Fort Worth, TX 76107	
Purgatory Pie Press*	212.274.8228	19 Hudson St., No. 403 New York, NY 10013 www.purgatorypiepress.com	hand letterpress, custom stationery
The Red Studio	323.465.2602	Los Angeles, CA	letterpress
Ross-Cook Engraving	212.563.2876	135 West 29th Street New York, NY 10001	full-service engraving, embossing & printing

Ruffles & Flourishes	509.627.5906	Richland, WA	molded paper stationery; call for local availability
Scriptura	504.897.1555	5423 Magazine St. New Orleans, LA 70115	
Silberman-Brown Stationers	206.292.9404	1322 Fifth Ave. Seattle, WA 98101	invitations
SoHo Letterpress	212.334.4356	71 Greene St. New York, NY 10012	custom stationery, printing, graphic design, letterpress
Soho Reprographics	212.925.7575	48 Greene St. New York, NY 10012	custom stationery
Solum World Paper	650.812.7584	Palo Alto, CA www.solum.com	imported printed papers
Soolip Paperie & Press	310.360.0545	8646 Melrose Ave. West Hollywood, CA 90069	
Stampworks 2000	212.679.5370	36 East 29th Street New York, NY 10012	custom rubber stamps
Studio Z Mendocino*	707.964.2522	Fort Bragg, CA www.studio-z.com	letterpress stationery
Twelve Dozen Graphics*	617.363.9783	Boston, MA	custom invitations, graphic design
Uptown Rubber Stamps	970.493.3212 800.888.3212	Ft. Collins, CO	
Visual Miracles	212.691.4491	55 West 19th Street New York, NY	color laser copy center
Viviano Design*	503.973.6538	Portland, OR www.vivianodesign.com	graphic design
The Wolf Paper & Twine Co.	212.675.4870	680 Sixth Avenue New York, NY 10010	craft paper, tissues
Write Selection	214.750.0531	314 Preston Royal Village Dallas, TX 75230	
Zorn Design Studio	213.344.9995	1800 Diamond Ave. S. Pasadena, CA 91030	

TABLEWARE

NAME	PHONE	ADDRESS	COMMENTS
Abigails*	800.678.8485 318.448.4695	Alexandria, LA	glassware and ceramics
Annie Glass	800.729.7350	109 Coopers Street Santa Cruz, CA 95060 www.annieglass.com	glassware
Arc International*	800.257.7470 609.825.5620	Millville, NJ	crystal stemware
Artel at Metropolitan Design Group	212.944.6110	New York, NY	etched glassware
Asiaphile*	818.550.1450	Glendale, CA	laquerware
Bernardaud*	800.884.7775	499 Park Avenue New York, NY 10022 www.bernardaud.fr	Limoges porcelain, bridal registry
Buccellati	212.308.2900 310.276.7022	New York, NY Beverly Hills, NY	Italian sterling flatware, gifts
C.E. Corey	516.997.9163	Old Westbury, NY	floral patterned porcelain
CFC - Daum	212.481.0288	New York, NY	fine crystal
Camden Lane	212.989.6813	New York, NY	collection representative
Carnevale*	800.548.9979 901.775.0800	Memphis, TN	silver chalices laquerware
Daniel Levy Ceramics*	212.268.0878	New York, NY	contemporary porcelain custom designs
Dansk International Designs LTD.*	800.293.2675 609.896.2800	White Plains, NY www.dansk.com	glass and pewter a specialty
Davis & Guiterrez	208.331.3792	Boise, ID	colorful glassware
Dickey Glass & Co.*	800.860.4527	Williamstown, WV	glassware to order, dozens color options

Dish Is	888.895.8911 212.352.9051	143 West 22nd Street New York, NY	
Eastern Accent International Inc.*	978.443.4308	Sudbury, MA	hand-etched glassware
Ebeling & Reuss	800.843.9551 610.366.8304	Allentown, PA	chintz porcelain
The End of History	212.647.7598	548 ½ Hudson Street New York, NY	mid-20th-century accessories
Fishs Eddy	877.347.4733 212.420.9020	889 Broadway New York, NY 10003	restaurant ware, industrial china
Gense*	888.368.4360 212.725.2882	New York, NY	sterling flatware
Hoffman's Patterns of the Past	888.559.5335 815.875.1944	Princeton, IL	discontinued china a specialty
Hogund Glass	201.985.0709	Jersey City, NJ	New Zealand artisans
Hôtel	203.655.4252	Darien, CT	European hotel silver
Jill Rosenwald*	617.422.0787	Boston, MA	ceramics
Jonathan Adler	212.941.8950	465 Broome Street New York, NY 10013	contemporary pottery
Kathy Erteman	212.929.3970	New York, NY	ceramic vessels
Kim Seybert	212.564.7850	New York, NY	glass bead coasters
Lalique*	800.993.2580 212.684.6760	712 Madison Avenue New York, NY www.lalique.com	fine crystal
Lenox Brands*	800.635.3669 609.844.1467	Lawrenceville, NJ www.lenox.com	china, crystal. silver
LouLou's Lost and Found	617.859.8593	121 Newbury Street Boston, MA 02116	hotel silver
Mariposa	800.788.1304	Manchester, MA	enameled flatware a specialty

R E S O

Michael C. Fina*	800.289.3462	New York, NY	china, crystal, sterling
Mottaheda	212.685.3050	New York, NY	Majolica; blue & white
Nan Swid*	212.633.6699	New York, NY	lusterware
Once Upon a Table	413.443.6622	30 Crofut St. Pittsfield, MA 01201 www.onceuponatable.com	vintage kitchen and tableware
Ostafin Designs*	212.352.9210	New York, NY	vintage Limoge, glassware
Potluck Studios*	914.626.2300	23 Main Street Accord, NY 12404	ceramics
Reed & Barton	800.822.1824	Taunton, MA www.reedbarton.com	sterling, pewter flatware, tableware
Replacements Limited	800.REPLACE	McLeansville, NC	hard-to-find china, discontinued china
Romancing Provence	212.481.9879	New York, NY www.romancingprovence.com	
Rosenthal USA	800.804.8070 201.804.8000	Carlstadt, NJ	crystal, china, flatware
Simon Pearce*	212.334.2393 802.295.2711	120 Wooster Street New York, NY The Mill Quechee, VT www.simonpearce.com	fine hand-blown glass
Smith & Co	415.621.8608	San Francisco, CA	pewter plates, tankards, candlesticks
Stupell Fine Gifts	212.260.3100	29 East 22nd Street New York, NY 10010	china, crystal, flatware
Square One	800.316.8080	Tampa, FL	vibrant patterned plates
Table Decor International	800.265.5267 770.432.1156	Marietta, GA www.tabledecor.com	custom monogramming
Tampopo*	888.826.7676 415.436.9200	55 Potrero Avenue San Francisco, CA 94103	Japanese tabletop accessories

Tea For Two	949.494.7776	Laguna Beach, CA	
Towle	617.561.2200	East Boston, MA	sterling, silver plate flatware
Trudy Borenstein	609.683.7831	Princeton, NJ	sterling accessories
Tudor Rose Antiques	212.677.5239	New York, NY	sterling tableware, gifts
Villa Ceramica	203.866.6399	South Norwalk, CT	Majolica
Wallace Silversmiths*	617.561.2200	East Boston, MA	sterling flatware, service

TRANSPORTATION

NAME	PHONE	ADDRESS	COMMENTS
Academy Bus Tours	201.420.7000	Hoboken, NJ www.academybus.com	luxury coaches
Antique Autos	310.323.9028	8306 Wilshire Blvd. Beverly Hills, CA 90212	
Bamboo Bike Co.	503.650.5162	West Linn, OR www.bamboobike.com	
Beverly Hills Car Collection	800.729.7350	Beverly Hills, CA	luxury car rentals
Black Tie Limo	631.698.9667 718.449.4162	Farmingville, NY www.blacktielimoeast.com	brochure
Bonaventure Hot Air Balloons	707.944.2822	Napa, CA www.bonaventuraballons.com	brochure
The Border Bus	214.855.0296	1801 N. Lamar Blvd. Dallas, TX 75202	decorated charter bus
Budget	800.527.0700	www.budget.com	luxury car rentals by special order
Carey International Limousine Service	800.336.4646	Washington, DC	chauffeured limousines booked nationally

R E S O

Cars of Yesterday	973.334.7663	Boonton, NJ	vintage rentals
Cartwright Ranch & Stables	817.249.2490	Fort Worth, TX	horse-drawn carriages
Chateau Stables Inc.	212.246.0520	New York, NY www.chateaustables.com	horse-drawn carriages
Classic Car Suppliers	310.657.7823	1905 Sunset Plaza Dr. W. Hollywood, CA 90069	
Colonial Parking	302.651.3600	Wilmington, DE	valet service
Dav-El	800.922.0343		chauffeured transportation network
Doubletree Farms	214.631.4096	Dallas, TX	horse-drawn carriages, wagons
Express Valet Parking	800.522.8156	Los Angeles, CA	
Five Star Limousines of Texas	214.630.9444	Dallas, TX	limousines and Rolls-Royces
Gaslight Limos	718.338.5374		antique autos
Integrated Transportation Services	800.ITS.4.ALL	Beverly Hills, CA www.itslimo.com	chauffeured limousines
Lifestyle Transportations	617.381.0600	2 Betty St. Everett, MA 02149	
McKinney Transit Authority	214.855.0006	3155 Oak Grove Dallas, TX 75204	trolley cars for charter through historic and arts districts of Dallas
Meyer Valet Parking	800.VALET.PK	New Rochelle, NY	uniformed attendants
Mogel's Classic Autos	909.622.1617	Pomona, CA	chauffeured antiques, vintage sports cars
Napa Valley Model A Rentals	707.944.1106	Yountville, CA	reproduction antique autos

New York Pedicabs	212.996.9436	434 East 89th Street New York, NY 10128	chauffeur-pedaled tricycle-cabs
Shamrocks Carriages	414.272.6873	Milwaukee, WI	
Superior Location Van Service	201.579.7374 800.888.3488	Newton, NJ Miami, FL	location van rentals, location finder
Town Limousines	201.939.7477	Lyndhurst, NJ www.townlimo.daweb.com	Rolls Royce for rent
Yellow Rose Carriages	317.634.3400	Indianapolis, IN	horse-drawn vehicles

WEDDING CAKES

NAME	PHONE	ADDRESS	COMMENTS
Ana Paz Cakes	305.471.5850	1460 NW 107th Ave., Unit D Miami, FL 33172	custom designer
Ann Amernick	301.718.0434	Chevy Chase, MD	
Ashley Bakery	843.763.4125	Charleston, SC	
Beth Hirsch	212.941.8085	New York, NY	miniature cakes
Betty van Norstrand	914.471.3386	Poughkeepsie, NY	miniature sugar work a specialty
Bijoux Doux*	212.226.0948	New York, NY	
Cake and Cookies by Maria	610.767.7109	Walnutport, PA	custom cakes
Cake Decorating by Toba*	212.234.3635	New York, NY	baker: winter chapter
The Cakery	303.797.7418	5151 S. Federal Blvd. Littleton, CO 80203	fondant a specialty

R   E   S   O

Cakework	415.821.1333	San Francisco, CA www.cakework.com	
The Cakeworks*	213.934.6515	Los Angeles, CA	tromp l'oeil portraits; by appointment
Carol Schmidt	504.888.2049	Metairie, LA	
Chantilly	718.859.1110	Brooklyn, NY	kosher cakes
Cheryl Kleinman	718.237.2271	Brooklyn, NY.	baker: spring chapter
Classic Cakes	317.844.6901	Indianapolis, IN	
Classic Cakes and Pastries	860.586.8202	Manchester, CT	
Colette's Cakes	212.366.6530	New York, NY	author, wedding cake cookbooks
Cravings	314.961.3534	8149 Big Bend Welster Groves, MO 63119	buttercream a specialty
Culinary Institute of America	914.452.9600	Hyde Park, NY www.ciachef.edu	
Debra Yates	816.587.1095	5418 NW Venetian Dr. Kansas City, MO 64151	marzipan a specialty
Daniels Bakery	940.322.4043	Witchita Falls, TX	
Debra Yates	816.587.1095	Kansas City, MO	marzipan a specialty
Donald Wressel*	310.273.2222	Los Angeles, CA	The Four Seasons pastry chef; spun sugar a specialty
Duane Park Patisserie	888.274.8447	179 Duane Street New York, NY 10013 www.madelines.net	classic French & Viennese desserts, croquembouche
Edible Work of Art	312.895.2200	Chicago, IL	
Fantasy Frostings	562.941.6266 800.649.0243	Whittier, CA	
FJ Pastries	212.614.9054	New York, NY	fondants petit fours

Food Attitude	212.686.4644	235 East 25th Street New York, NY www.weddingcakeonline.com	cakes available on a week's notice
Frosted Art by Arturo Diaz	214.760.8707	1546 Edison St. Dallas, TX 75207	pastillage flowers, grooms' cakes
Gail Watson Custom Cakes*	212.967.9167	335 W. 38th St. New York, NY 10018 www.gailwatsoncake.com	
Hansen Cakes	213.936.4332	1072 S. Fairfax Ave. Los Angeles, CA 90019	
Hirsch Baking	212.941.8085	New York, NY	small custom bakery
Isn't That Special- Outrageous Cakes	201.216.0123	Hoboken, NJ	afrocentric motifs a specialty
Jan Kish	614.848.5855	Worthington, OH	
Jan's Cakes	831.423.4481	Davenport, CA	
Jane Stacey	505.473.1243	2092 Calle Contento Santa Fe, NM 87505	custom designs
John and Mike's Amazing Cakes*	206.869.2992	14934 NE 31st Circle Redmond, WA 98052	architectural and theme cakes
John Paul	843.744.6791	Charleston, SC	
Katrina Rozelle Pastries and Desserts	925.837.6337	Alamo, CA	
Le Gateau Cakery	214.528.6102	3128 Harvard Dallas, TX 75205	
Le Royale Icing by Margaret Lastick	708.386.4175	35 Chicago Ave. Oak Park, IL 60302	custom cakes
Les Friandises	212.988.1616	972 Lexington Ave. New York, NY 10021	patisserie
Margaret Braun*	212.929.1582	New York, NY	baker: summer chapter
Marjolaine	408.867.2226 650.949.2226	Saratoga, CA	

R   E   S   O

Michel Richard	310.275.5707	310 S. Robertson Blvd. Los Angeles, CA 90048	
Mike's Amazing Cakes	425.869.2992	Redmond, WA	novelties a specialty
MIM Fine Pastries	914.265.2328	Garrison, NY	water color style painting on fondant
Patisserie J. Lanciani	212.989.1213	414 West 14th Street New York, NY 10014	
Patticakes	818.794.1128	1900 N. Allen Ave. Altadena, CA 91001	
Polly's Cakes*	503.230.1986	Portland, OR www.polly'scakes	custom cakes; by appointment
A Piece of Cake	843.881.2034	Charleston, SC	
Ron Ben-Israel	212.627.2418	New York, NY	
Rosie's Creations,	212.362.6069	New York, NY	keepsakes and cookies
Rosemary Watson	800.203.0629 201.538.3542	Morristown, NJ	custom cakes, lace mold detailing; mail order
Rosemary's Cakes*	201.833.2417 305.932.2989	Teaneck, NJ	baker: fall chapter
Royale Icing Custom Cakes	708.386.4175	Oak Park, IL www.royaleicing.com	custom cakes, buttercream
Sima's	414.257.0998	817 N. 68th St. Milwaukee, WI 53213	
A Spirited Cake	214.522.2212	3014 Montecello Dallas, TX 75205	
Steven Kic*	703.848.0028	McLean, VA www.pastryarts.com	chocolatier
SUD Fine Pastry and Cafe	215.592.0499	Philadelphia, PA	custom cakes, pastries, molded flowers
Susan Kennedy Chopson	615.865.2437	644 Delaware Ave. Madison, TN 37115	

Sylvia Weinstock Cakes	212.925.6698	273 Church St. New York, NY 10013	by appointment
A Taste of Europe by Gisela	817.654.9494	4817 Brentwood Stair Fort Worth, TX 76103	
Three Tarts Bakery & Cafe	847.446.5444	Northfield, IL	
Victoria's Fancy Wedding Cakes	320.352.2636	417 North Oak St. Sauk Centre, MN 56378	royal icing a specialty

WINES & SPIRITS

NAME	PHONE	ADDRESS	COMMENTS
Ale-in-the-Mail	800.573.6325	Plainview, NY	microbrews by mail, gift packages
Best Cellars	212.426.4200	1291 Lexington Ave. New York, NY 10128 www.bestcellars.com	wines under $10
Champion	206.284.8306	108 Denny Way Seattle, WA 98109	local wines by mail
Domaine Carneros by Taittinger	707.257.0101	Napa, CA www.domainecarneros.com	private tours & tastings
D. Sokolin	631.283.0505	Southampton, NY	fine wines
Du Vin	310.855.1161	Los Angeles, CA	
Hog's Head Beer Cellars	336.333.2337	Greensboro, NC www.hogshead.com	brewed beer gift packages
International Wine Center	212.268.7517	New York, NY	tastings, classes
Kobrand Wine	800.628.2921	New York, NY	Champagne selecting; distributors of Taittinger, Domaine Carneros

Kreston Liquors	302.652.3792	904 Concord Ave. Wilmington, DE 19802	wine, Champagne, spirits, beer, ice; event consultation
Marty's	214.526.7796	3316 Oak Lane Dallas, TX 75219	
Moore Brothers Wine Company	856.317.1177	71200 North Park Dr. Pennsauken, NJ www.moore.bros.com	unusual wines a specialty
Morrell & Co.	800.96.WINES	New York, NY www.morrelandco.com	fine wines
Partners in Wine	734.761.2333	615 S. Main St. Ann Arbor, MI 48104	
Sherry-Lehmann	212.838.7500	679 Madison Ave. New York, NY 10022 www.sherry-lehmann.com	fine wines, Champagne; catalog
Tony's Wine Warehouse	214.520.9463	2904 Oak Lawn Dallas, TX 75219	
Windsor Wines	212.779.4422	New York, NY